HOW
–not to–
DATE

Judy McGuire

SASQUATCH BOOKS
SEATTLE

Printed in the United States of America
Published by Sasquatch Books
Distributed by PGW/Perseus
15 14 13 12 11 10 09 08 07   9 8 7 6 5 4 3 2 1

Cover design: Rosebud Eustace
Interior design: Stewart A. Williams/Sarah Plein
Interior composition: Sarah Plein

Library of Congress Cataloging-in-Publication Data
McGuire, Judy.
  How not to date / Judy McGuire.
     p. cm.
  ISBN-13: 978-1-57061-532-0
  ISBN-10: 1-57061-532-2
  1. Dating (Social customs) 2. Women--Psychology. 3. Men--Psychology. I. Title.

HQ801.M487723 2007
306.73--dc22

                            2007032561

Sasquatch Books
119 South Main Street, Suite 400
Seattle, WA 98104
(206) 467-4300
www.sasquatchbooks.com
custserv@sasquatchbooks.com

*For my mom, who knew I'd be a writer
before I did.**

**But Mom, if they have reading where you are, please skip
pages 14, 52, and 73. Oh, and 106, 123, and 190–193, too.*

PART **1**

WORRIED GRIMACE ~ 1

The Fashion Victim 8

Oooh, That Smell! 11

Liar, Liar, Pants on Fire—The Shallow End 17

Three's a Crowd 22

Not Quite My Type 25

Painfully Shy 30

The Cheapskate, Level I 34

The Crazy, Level I 37

How to Extricate Yourself 38

PART **2**

ONE EYEBROW RAISED ~ 41

Rude Boy (or Girl), or Say It, Don't Spray It:
   Adventures in Bad Manners 45

Dating on the Wrong Team 48

The Oversharer 53

The Idiot 58

The Mope 65

Would You Like Some Crackers with Your Cheese? 69

The Bad Kisser! 71

The Cheapskate, Level II 75

Liar, Liar, Pants on Fire—Adult Swim 81

What Not to Say (Specifically) 85

PART **3**

BOTH EYEBROWS FURROWED IN HORROR ~ 89

Hi, I'm Inappropriate! 94

I Love You—What Was Your Name? 99

Politically Incorrect 103

The Leg Humper 109

Are We Having Whine with Dinner? 117

The Self-Promoter 125

The Critic 129

The Crazy, Level II 132

The Cheapstake, Level III 137

PART **4**

ABANDON HOPE ALL YE WHO ENTER HERE ~ 141

Gross! 144

Bad Boys (and Girls) 148

DOA (Drunk on Arrival) 159

The Face of Evil 165

I'm Mad and I'm Not Going to Take It Anymore:
   Adventures in Dating the Terminally Angry 172

The Gun Jumper 175

The Cheapskate, Level IV 177

The Consolation Date 179

The Crazy, Level III 185

The Incontinent 187

Liar, Liar, Pants on Fire—The Deep End 194

Afterword   199

Acknowledgments   201

INTRODUCTION

When I was about 4 years old, my parents invited Father Hermley, the priest who'd married them, over to our house so he could meet their rapidly expanding family. (I was and remain the eldest of five.) Father Hermley seemed very interested in getting to know me and pulled me up onto his lap. Even decades later, I recall not enjoying this one bit.

Though I can't recall his exact words, I remember the Father asking me a great many questions about myself, my feelings, and my thoughts on God. Did I mention I was 4 at the time? I squirmed uncomfortably and answered like any aspiring wiseass would—basically, I made fun. Of a priest. The same priest who'd joined my mom and dad in holy matrimony.

Being a tad humor-impaired, Father Hermley wasn't a bit amused by my toddler high jinks and gravely diagnosed me "a very negative person." As I was only 4, I had no idea what this meant, but I could tell by the grimace on my mortified mom's face that whatever it was, it wasn't good.

And so, for the rest of her life, whenever we got into an argument—and there were puh-lenty of those—her closing zinger would be a hissed "Father Hermley was right!"

As it turns out, he was. Despite reading countless how-to books, I've always found learning by negative example to be a far more effective (not to mention entertaining) method. I'm not the only one. For example, you can tell a child not to touch the stove, but let little Johnny go ahead and fondle that burner, and you'll never have to waste another breath on the topic. Of course there may be an emergency room visit in your future, but this book is about dating. If you are experiencing medical emergencies during your dates, you probably need more than a book.

Using the same logic, you can advise that a person refrain from dating a 35-year-old alcoholic who lives on his grandmother's cat hair–coated sofa, but wouldn't Grandma walking in on the two of you experimenting with female ejaculation be a far more effective deterrent? See where I'm going here?

During my seven-plus-year tenure as a sex and love advice columnist—the majority of which I spent single—I've either experienced firsthand or read about dates so heinous it's truly a wonder my vagina didn't seal itself shut. There were dark days, when dating seemed like a minefield—round every corner lurked some emotional terrorist, waiting to break my heart and stiff me with the check. After a lot of missteps and mistakes, I eventually learned to navigate what I hesitantly call the dating game with varying degrees of success.

And sure, while other so-called sexperts might have things like degrees to prove they're qualified for the job, I have something more valuable—something hard-won and not necessarily pleasant. What I'm talking about is experience. Do you think Dr. Phil ever watched as a crush hit on his friend? Pffft . . . I think not. But look at Dear Abby and Ann Landers—two advice-doling sisters with zero in the way of professional qualifications, who went years without speaking to each other. Much like myself, those two embraced their dysfunction and used it to help others.

It wasn't like I set out to date weirdos and lowlifes exclusively, but for a while it sure seemed that way. Friends and family lost countless hours of sleep fretting over me and wondering when and where the freak magnet had been implanted. I could be dropped into a room packed with nothing but perfectly sane men with jobs, and I would gravitate toward the one guy everyone else was trying to avoid:

the unemployed know-it-all with the chronic case of pso-riasis and a highly unsavory yen for his little sister (in his defense, she was a half sister).

So yes, maybe instead of field research, I should've par-layed my criminology BA into a PhD at some prestigious uni-versity, but who are you going to feel more comfortable taking advice from—some married lady with an office and a framed piece of paper, or a dame who's been floundering about in the dating pool for years?

See, I thought so!

But even as prolific a dater as I was, one person's expe-riences do not a book make. So, utilizing highly unscien-tific research methods, I (mostly) ignored the experts and headed straight into the trenches to talk with others on the front line . . . those brave and resilient soldiers . . . my fel-low daters.

What I found may shock you. It may also repulse you, impugn your faith in humankind and/or cause you to con-sider a life of celibacy. What I have discovered is that, contrary to what you might believe, not all bad dates are created equal. Nor does a rotten first date mean there won't necessarily be another one. Generally—but not always—a less-than-glowing first impression leads to a downright horrifying second one, but as with all things, there are the rare exceptions to this rule.

Not surprisingly, different daters have different deal breakers. For some, a seemingly minor violation, such as an inadvertent butt squeak or runaway nose hair, might spell the end. Others can live with questionable hygiene and unpleasant aromas but run shrieking when confronted with a fanny pack or ill-fitting velour tracksuit.

What I've attempted to uncover are the universals— things most sane daters would have an issue with—and organize them into groups. Not only that, but when called for, I'll also tell you how to extricate yourself from situations gone horribly wrong.

Because, as Pat Benatar once wisely crooned, "Love is a battlefield," I decided to use the U.S. government's threat advisory scale as inspiration. I've organized and categorized the varieties of bad dates according to escalating levels of heinousness.

What I couldn't do is abide by the government's color scheme. Red, orange, yellow, blue, and green? Boooring. Surely there must exist a more vibrant palette than that! I looked around my apartment. Magenta kitchen; blood-red living room; cool, Caribbean blue bathroom . . . hmm. Still, somehow not right. Then my eyes landed upon a cheery little magazine stuffed under a stack of unpaid bills. The J. Crew catalog! I thumbed through and got more excited every page. No primary colors for these folks, no siree! Where I saw yellowy-brown, they saw "ochre." In the magical world of J. Crew green becomes "deep elm," pink is actually "flamingo." So much more glam, so much more me!

So behold, the *How Not to Date* threat advisory chart—in ascending order of awfulness:

- **PALE SURPLUS**: The color beige, or, as the arbiters of preppy style at J. Crew renamed it, "Pale Surplus," is synonymous with a few other "B" words: boring, bland, and banal. There's nothing really wrong with a date you'd categorize as pale surplus, but there's nothing particularly right about it either. Like a boring outfit that can be snazzed up with some festive accessories, this date had better come up with something interesting fast.

- **GERANIUM (AN UNPLEASANT ORANGE)**: The geranium date takes the unpleasant up a notch. Maybe it's the way she smells, perhaps it's the way she calls you "Daddy," but unless she starts sneezing dollar bills, you're probably not going to go out with her again.

- **ENDIVE (AKA KAOPECTATE GREEN):** Who hasn't been out on a date that's so bad you start looking around for the hidden cameras? There's only one reason to stick around for a date like this, and that's so you can entertain your friends with the tale later.

- **CAROB (OTHERWISE KNOWN AS FAUX CHOCO-LATE):** Remember being a little kid and mistaking mom's unsweetened baking chocolate for a Hershey bar? Much like that bitter, foul-tasting stuff, this date may appear palatable at first glance, but upon doing the metaphorical taste test, you're left with no choice but to spit and run.

My plan is that this book will make you laugh and maybe help you get a little better at selecting who to waste your time on. Hopefully it'll make you feel less alone and realize that bad dates don't only happen to bad people—a crappy night out can happen to anyone. And, hey, even if there's nothing in this book that you can remotely relate to, at least it'll leave you with a yummy warm feeling of smug superiority.

PART ONE

WORRIED GRIMACE

THREAT LEVEL: PALE SURPLUS

Had two husbands; one was too short, one was gay. Still sweetie, if you want to know how to peck a dwarf on the cheek as he's walking out of the house to the disco in your dress, then I'm your girl.

—EDINA MONSOON, *ABSOLUTELY FABULOUS*

PART ONE: WORRIED GRIMACE

THREAT LEVEL: PALE SURPLUS

Any experienced dater has had at least one or two spectacularly bad dates. Those unenchanted evenings that just keep spiraling downward and careening out of control. You hate him. He loathes you. Things just keep getting worse until you wind up either shrieking at each other or waking your mom up for bail money.

But most rotten dates don't end in such fireworks. Instead, you're forced to suffer through a long, slow fizzle. The awkward silences. The forced laughter. The fervent wishing for spontaneous combustion (on your date's part, naturally).

Depending on where you are in the dating spectrum, these going-nowhere-verrrrry-slowly assignations can actually be more soul crushing than the pyrotechnic car-crash variety, because what you're experiencing is so just-plain-disheartening that you don't even have energy enough to hate the other person; you just wish they would evaporate into the ether.

At least if the person is truly repellent you have an entertaining story for your friends: "He picked his nose, wiped it on the wall, and acted like nothing had happened!" or "She burst into tears as the waiter recited the specials because she spent fourth grade in special ed!" Those dates—which we'll cover at great length in Parts Two through Four—can actually be kind of fun; darkly hilarious like a John Waters movie.

The Pale Surplus date runs more along the lines of Swedish existential cinema. There are no giggles, no shy blushes, and most of all, no fun. (I suppose you could look at the bright side in that nobody scarfs down a dog turd either.) Instead you're stuck staring at a not-so-special someone as they drone on, and you do your best to feign interest. Your Pale Surplus accomplice may be perfectly nice, but they're also just wrong. Not a dangerous, exciting kind of wrong; more just wrong for you. The old adage says that every pot has its lid, so no doubt somewhere there's a guy or gal out there who'll find tales of misplaced file folders and alphabetizing gone horribly awry endlessly fascinating. But that special person isn't you.

You're about ready to poke your own eye out to interject a little excitement into the evening, but at the same time, this person's offense is not egregious enough to feign food poisoning over. They're not *horrible*, so you can't just make a run for it. And so you sit. Sit and pretend to listen until enough time has passed that you can safely excuse yourself with no worry of recriminations of rudeness.

While life holds no guarantees, there are measures one can take to lessen the chances of winding up on a one-way date to Dullsville (or worse)—see the sidebar on p. 6.

But even elimi-dating the virulently unsuitable doesn't guarantee an evening of scintillating conversation and furtive feel-ups. I can't count how many times a guy looked great on paper—or, more likely, online—only to have him show up and be a dud spud in the flesh. Chemistry is an elusive thing. It can ignite feelings you'd forgotten you could even have or stir up emotions that could quite possibly get you arrested. In Part One, we'll explore the less explosive combinations.

The Do Not Call List, or, Who Not to Date

To help weed out the guaranteed dating disasters, I've concocted a list of potential dates guaranteed to be more trouble than they're worth:

• **YOUR FRIEND'S EX.** Remember on *90210* when Brenda found out Dylan was putting it to her best bud, Kelly? Ugly, right? Unless you have received written permission from your pal, your friend's ex is off-limits. Even if your friend is OK with it, it's guaranteed that the specter of your friend will loom large on this outing, and everyone knows that three's a crowd. (Unless you're polyamorous, but I'm keeping things simple here.) It's bad enough hearing about exes you don't know—do you really want to discover that your yoga partner can only reach orgasm by being manipulated "down there" with a bottle cap.

• **YOUR FRIEND'S CURRENT.** This is so shitty I'm not even going to explain why.

• **ANYONE YOU MET IN REHAB . . .** While it's nice to have things in common, a shared fondness for pharmaceuticals does not a love connection make.

• **. . . OR PRISON.** Yes, you both paid your debt to society, but you're out now. Time to quit cavorting with criminals.

• **THE GUY/GAL IN THE NEXT CUBICLE—THOUGH DOWN THE HALL AND AROUND THE CORNER IS JUST FINE.** We all know we're not supposed to date people we work with, but pretty much everyone I know has ignored this at one point or another. Just do your co-workers a favor and keep it clean from nine to five; nobody needs to know that Stan from accounting favors boxers over briefs.

• **YOUR IT GUY/GIRL.** Besides your boss or a subordinate, the one person you should absolutely avoid getting naked with is your office's information technology professional. These peeps have the power to see and read anything and everything on your computer. But then, maybe you're comfortable with that. Ahem.

• **THE CRUSH FROM DAYS PAST.** When unrequited crushes come back into the picture long after you've gotten over them, it's tempting to go see what might've been. Don't. These scenarios never end well. Trust me.

• **THE DREADED EX.** While it's a given that nine times out of ten you will break down and have sex with an ex, don't blow it up into anything more than an isolated incident. Nobody likes a repeat. Especially the friends who listened to you bitch and moan the first time around.

THE FASHION VICTIM

The first time I met Lou, an ex who carries the distinction of being my most long-term relationship to date, there was a fanny pack carefully threaded through the belt loops of his pleated trousers and a long, skinny rattail wending its way down his back. I took one look and snottily declared—to the other voices in my head—"rock critic." While Lou eventually started to grow on me, his sartorial missteps remained an issue. Albeit one I learned to live with.

But not every girl is as forgiving as *moi*. Jen Dziura, a 30-year-old NYC comedian, never knew her limits until she was confronted with a date's unusual take on bling. "I met this guy in front of a bar in the East Village—he was a Ukrainian hip-hop DJ," she told me. "Under the dim light of the street lamps, I noticed something a little strange about his bottom teeth. Although they possessed a peculiar dark sheen, they also seemed to . . . glisten."

Curious, Jen agreed to have a drink with the guy. "It was even darker inside the bar, and I was still trying to figure out the mystery of the teeth. I thought perhaps this was a work of budget dentistry; maybe if you lose an entire row of teeth in the Ukraine, you get them replaced with stainless steel. Finally he asked, 'Do my fronts bother you?'"

Like me, white-girl Jen had no idea what he was talking about.

"Your what?"

"My fronts, you don't like them?"

"I had never seen a white guy wearing fronts. I had never seen a whole row of bottom fronts, and they weren't gold, but kind of a dull silver—like pewter." Jen stared, perplexed.

"Look over there!" the DJ yelped, cleverly creating a diversion by pointing toward the bar. As Jen turned to look, this charming fella spat the dubious dental accessories into his hand and slid them into his pocket.

But sometimes a fashion faux pas is more than just a visual assault on the senses. Turns out, in some cases you *can* judge a book by its cover, as Kate C., a 33-year-old editor from New York, once found out. "It was a Nerve.com date I went on the week after 9/11. This girl—I think her name was Brenda—showed up with an American flag bandana on her head," the still-horrified copy jockey shared. And that wasn't all. "As soon as she sat down, she started ranting about killing Arabs. What else can you really say about that?"

What, indeed.

Through countless interviews with seasoned daters, I discovered one interesting fact about dating the unfashionable: while most ladies I spoke with rattled off long lists of style violations—designer jeans on men, tie-dyed anything, hemp clothing and/or jewelry, do-rags—it seems men pretty much don't care what their date is wearing. Until they get involved with you anyway. Informal research has shown that most men are drawn to slutty-looking broads. Short skirts, low-cut shirts—it's all good when they're just scoping you out at the bar. But once things take a turn for the serious, most guys will expect the flashy dame to tone it down and lower the hemlines.

WHAT YOU HAVE TO LOOK FORWARD TO

We ladies are always thinking we can "fix" even the most egregious fashion fatality. "Surely, once he gets a taste of my loving, he'll discard the Members Only jacket and MC Hammer pants," we tell ourselves. And the fact is, we're mostly correct. Men are far more likely to change the way they dress than women are, especially if you buy the stuff for them and offer positive reinforcement (blow jobs) when they finally toss the baseball hat with built-in beer can holder in the trash. Women tend to be more attached to their look, so you'd best prepare your mom for the chance that your date for Christmas dinner may show up wearing a visible thong and Lee Press On nails.

OOOH, THAT SMELL!

N ed had messy bleach blond hair, giant bright blue eyes, and the air of a lost little puppy. Like most women, I found this sort of hapless forlornness appealing at a certain point in my life. Unfortunately, Ned was also so hygiene-impaired that I regularly made him leave his shoes out on the fire escape when he came for sleepover visits. Ned was a vegan and fancied himself an anarchist punk rocker. Translation: He got all sanctimonious if I dared to eat meat in front of him, and believe me, I dared. Because leather was off-limits, he wore vinyl pants instead. Do you have any idea how gnarly sweaty vinyl smells? No? I'll do you a favor and spare you the description.

What Not to Wear

Though it's true that people come in all shapes and sizes, and what looks good on one person can turn another into a dead ringer for a thrift-store mannequin, there are some universal fashion don'ts that every human being should heed.

• **PLEATED PANTS.** If you're skinny, you'll look lumpy; if you're already packing a few extra pounds . . . wide load ahead!

• **BASEBALL CAP.** Unless you're actually planning to go nine innings on your outing, leave the cap at home. If you actually *are* doing something sporty, do not, under any circumstances, wear it backward. Or worse, at a jaunty angle.

• **VISIBLE UNDERPANTS.** This goes for ladies and gents. Depending on your gender, either pull your pants up or buy some of those low-rider panties. Nobody wants to see what brand of scanty you're wearin'.

• **MANDALS.** Until you guys start doing the kind of foot maintenance we ladies do, you're not allowed to wear sandals. Men who exhibit their weird, hornlike toenails and furry hobbit toes are generally not men who are having a lot of sex. And no, adding a sock to the equation does not a shoe make.

• **DO-RAGS.** According to a brief, highly unscientific survey (that is, I asked several girlfriends over cocktails), "don't-rag" is more like it.

• **OVERLY SLUTTY ATTIRE.** There is nothing worse than showing up decked out like Dita Von Teese, only to find yourself at dinner with Elmer Fudd's cross-eyed brother. Ascertain chemistry *before* busting out the bustier.

• **THE BERET.** Monica Lewinsky or Pepé Le Pew—your call. Both of them wrong numbers.

• **BLING AROUND THE COLLAR OR ANYWHERE ELSE.** The only grill you should be rocking is the one on your patio.

• **EXCESSIVE PRODUCT.** Your hair shouldn't make crunching sounds when your date touches it. Gotti boys, I'm talking to you.

• **YOUR BLUETOOTH.** Fine if you're the Starfleet captain; otherwise, knock it off.

Normally I could cope with a smile (and some Bengay smeared under my nostrils), but one day, Ned's funk was so completely overwhelming, my eyes actually watered. The usually stoic Mabel the Cat buried herself in a pile of my comparatively sweet-smelling dirty laundry to escape the stench. My collection of spendy French floral candles didn't stand a chance against the Pigpen-like mist enveloping my date and permeating my apartment. Much to his annoyance, I suggested he shower. Instead of taking the hint, Self-Important Stinky Boy went on a long diatribe about how cleanliness was just another construct of the bourgeoisie, blah, blah, blah. SISB wound up his mini rant by asking why I would want to oppress him by forcing him to bathe.

"Because you expect me to put that smelly penis of yours in my mouth," was my matter-of-fact reply. I guess his anarcho-scruples were flexible enough to allow bourgie blow jobs because he quit arguing and began scouring down a tad more regularly.

Most ladies aren't as tolerant—or, perhaps, as desperate—as I. Mona G. was seeing someone she really liked a lot when her heart was broken by a dental don't.

"We'd been dating for about a month, when we went out to dinner and he got a little—but not *that* little—meaty piece of burger and bun stuck right between his front teeth," she reported. "At first I thought, 'Poor guy, that could happen to anyone.'" Which is true enough. Who *hasn't* had that happen? Mona thought she was doing the right thing, giving him subtle hints, but when her boyfriend failed to take action, she finally came right out and told him.

He shrugged but did nothing. "I let it go, figuring he was too polite to pick his teeth in public." Wrong.

"Anyway, we went back to my place—we didn't even turn on the lights. He excused himself to use my bathroom, where he had his own toothbrush," she continued. "He, um, slept over. [Translation: They did it!] I woke up. We smiled at each other, and he STILL HAD THAT PIECE OF BURGER IN HIS TEETH!!"

Mona dumped him on the spot.

Clarissa J. ran into a similar problem with a comely teacher she once romanced. "Cute little Hannah," she recalled wistfully. "So nice, so sweet—she had a turtle."

Along with a pet reptile, Hannah also possessed the breath of a Gila monster. "It was so foul that when I kissed her, I actually got nauseous!" Clarissa J. gave it her all and went out with the Breath Offender a couple more times.

"She smoked Parliaments, and I think that must've made it worse." Eventually, the stink got to be too much. "I broke up with her because of the breath, but I told her it wasn't working out. I couldn't tell her it made me physically ill to kiss her."

WHAT YOU HAVE TO LOOK FORWARD TO

If, like me, you're silly enough to ignore sanitary slacker-dom, you can watch as you morph into your mother. Do you really want to be in a relationship that requires you to nag about flossing? To turn into the kind of person who speaks almost exclusively in passive-aggressive dropped hints? ("Doesn't my hair smell nice? It's this new totally organic, vegan shampoo. You should try it!") Take it from me, you don't. If someone doesn't care enough about themselves to wipe down with soap and water a couple times a week, you can bet that they aren't capable of caring about you.

LIAR, LIAR, PANTS ON FIRE —THE SHALLOW END

B ack in the olden days, you'd stumble across a potential paramour at a party or a bar, or maybe even in the next cubicle. The two of you would exchange numbers and then set a day and time to enjoy a meal or coffee together. Though your memory of the initial meeting was maybe sometimes clouded by beer goggles, you basically knew what you were getting into ahead of time.

Not so with the advent of online dating. The lethal combo of spell-check and Photoshop makes it possible for even the biggest schleprock to appear literate and appealing. A skillful manipulator of words and images can easily turn his schlubby little George Costanza self into an online double for George Clooney. At least until you see him in person.

According to the best-selling book *Freakonomics*, the biggest advantage a male online dater could possess is economic, whereas women fare better if they're beautiful (double duh!). Which is why men are more apt to exaggerate their income, and women are more likely to subtract a few—or thirty—pounds.

If you're going to go the online route, it's best to realize that a few fibbers are an inevitability. Just off the top of my head, I recall the 35-year-old who turned out to be 45: "But I *look* 35" was his reasoning. Hmmm . . . not really. Then there was the "writer" who turned out to be a hedge fund manager. I still don't understand that one—why make yourself poorer than you are? He was followed by a virtual parade of 5′9″ fellas who all turned out to be more like 5′6″ and the screenwriter who turned out to be just another unemployed/broke guy. I could go on but I won't.

Though most common lies are fairly harmless—weight, height, income, and age—they're also pretty stupid, as they're only "true" until you meet the person in real life. Anne G., a Seattle-based writer, said, "Lying about height makes me crazy. It's not that I want a 6′ tall dude. Call me old-fashioned, but I'm just over dating a guy who's half my size." Kate C. also fell victim to a height hoax. "Even though my ad said I was only looking for ladies, one guy responded and we chatted via e-mail. He seemed nice, so I figured, what the hell? I'll go out with him," she laughed. "I met him and he was a foot and a half shorter than his profile said. A few inches, I could see, but a foot and a half? I'm not that tall, and he barely came up to my shoulder."

Adding a few inches and shaving a few pounds are irritating but seem fairly innocuous when you look at all the married peeps masquerading as singles online. But for the moment, we're talking about the low-level fibbers here. We'll cover the super-screwed-up lies in Part Four.

WHAT YOU HAVE TO LOOK FORWARD TO

Though they may be too old, short, or fat for you, these age, height, and weight Internet-based stretchers-of-the-truth aren't necessarily evil. So many online shoppers—I mean, daters—rule out perfectly acceptable prospects using arbitrary parameters that a lot of these folks are only inflating or deflating the truth (and their inseam) in order to widen their demographic. You will come across the occasional delusional psycho, but you could meet one of them on the bus.

High School Confidential

The cutest story I heard while researching this book came from John B., a 46-year-old LA-based actor. I'll let him tell it:

I was a junior in high school and my school gave us the day off so we could attend the college fair in Hartford. The fellow who drove us was driving his dad's spiffy red convertible. When we got to the fair, we pulled in behind these really cute blondes. They were way out of our league.

Anyway, I was feeling puckish and knew we wouldn't see them again, so I left a note—with my phone number—saying that a devilishly handsome guy in a red convertible wouldn't mind a date.

Incredibly, a couple nights later I get a phone call—her name was Samantha—saying she'd like to go out sometime. She was a cheerleader type, and I was a zitty little drama nerd. Certainly not the type of guy she was dating. I said yes, in my high-pitched voice, "OK, where can I get you?"

I didn't have a red convertible; what I had was a yellow, beat-down, four-door family sedan. I drove up to pick her up, and when she opened the door and saw it was me . . . well, I never saw someone's face fall like that.

I knew right off the bat that we were in trouble. She kept looking over my shoulder to see if her friends had set her up as a joke.

She was a smoker. I wasn't but started bumming cig- arettes off her. I smoked her whole pack on the way to the restaurant. We sat down at dinner, and I don't think we had anything in common—I was an actor who liked to read; she was a cheerleader and liked to surf. We quickly fell into silence.

Dinner was over and we were supposed to go see Black Sunday. *She was so gorgeous . . . and guys always have this part of them that thinks and hopes that maybe through some miracle she'll start to warm up. Pity sex . . . anything . . .*

I was walking behind her on the way to the car, and suddenly she stops and starts to sway. Then falls back- ward, and I catch her.

Once she'd recovered she turned to me and said, "I left my medication at home. I should probably go now."

I asked what medication it was. "It's for a condition I have," she told me. "I don't like to talk about it."

I kept thinking I should've dropped her. But up until the very end, I kept asking if she wanted to go out again.

THREE'S A CROWD

Let's meet at this Korean restaurant I like. I'll be sitting at the bar" was what the man I hope will be my last Internet date suggested for our first outing. I love me some Korean food, so it sounded like a plan. As a longtime veteran of the online dating game, I knew what worked and so I pulled on my shortest skirt and paired it with my inexplicably lucky blouse. I never did figure out why this particular shirt brought the boys in—it was baggy and sort of falling apart in places, but it was like catnip to the menfolk. Go figure.

Anyway, I walked in and there he was: 6′5″ of handsome. We said our hellos, and I slid up onto the empty barstool to his right. The bartender came right over. I was on the verge of ordering a drink when my date butts in to introduce us. "This is Larry," he said. That's nice, I thought. He knows the bartender. We shook hands and I ordered my drink.

As we started to chat, I noticed several faces seated nearby peering over at us expectantly. I looked at my new friend for some kind of explanation.

"This is Mike, Ola, and Matt," he offered. We—or more accurately, *I*—were surrounded. I was being checked out by no less than *four* of his friends!

Apparently nobody had bothered to inform my beliked that dates are traditionally between *two* people. Not two people and four of one party's nearest and dearest!

However, meeting a guy's drinking buddies pales in comparison to what happened to Kiki P. "I went on a date with this man, and during dinner he told me that his mom was checking me out from a table nearby." Um, his *mother*? Quickly realizing that this was not to be a love connection, Kiki walked over to his mom and introduced herself. "She was a very interesting woman. She was on Prozac . . . a lot of fun." Kiki shrugged, "I dismissed her son early and had some calvados with his mom. She confessed that her son was a closet case."

Meeting a date's family right off the bat can save a girl some time and heartache, but it's also a bit of a strain. Anne G. was surprised when a man she had just started seeing brought his 11-year-old along on their date. "I tried to be cool about it, like I always meet people with children," she told me. "But I don't have any kids in my life, so I don't know how to act with them," she said. "I was trying to be the cool friend, but it didn't matter. I couldn't interact with the kid anyway, because the two of them spent the whole dinner fighting." Anne later found out that the son had met a lot of his dad's dates, so by the time he met Anne he was sick to death of the meet and greet. She also gathered that daddy dearest was looking for more of a mommy-type situation than she was willing to entertain. Buh-bye!

OK, so we can agree that bringing friends and family along for what's supposed to be a romantic night out can be awkward. But again, Kate C. (is the C for "Crazymagnet"?) takes it one step beyond.

"It was yet another Internet date," she laughed into the phone. "With this hot chick—I don't even remember her name. We meet up for drinks in my neighborhood, and she shows up with another woman." Understandably, Kate found this rather strange. "They were both acting like they were playing a joke on me—laughing at weird times, looking at each other funny."

Frankly, this sounds more like being tortured in the locker room by mean junior high girls than a date. Kate agreed. "Eventually they admit that the other woman was the underage ex-girlfriend my date had been telling me about. I almost got up and left them with the check. But that was five years ago, and I was slightly more tolerant than I am now."

WHAT YOU HAVE TO LOOK FORWARD TO

Group activities. Lots and lots of group activities—with family, with friends . . . Prepare to spend minimal time alone. Even today, my boyfriend—he of the four-friends-along—thinks nothing sounds like more fun than taking a vacation with ten of our closest pals. And he can keep on imagining that, because for as long as I'm in the picture he'll never know.

NOT QUITE MY TYPE

Cliff had a nasal voice and a tendency to gesticulate wildly. I wasn't attracted to him, but it's not every day that an art history professor offers to walk you through the Metropolitan Museum of Art. Our afternoon together was chaste but ultimately fairly informative—for me anyway. I don't know if he got anything out of it. I had to guess I was equally not his type, as I never heard another peep outta him after we said our good-byes.

Short, nebbishy Jeff was very sweet and treated me like a princess, which is probably why I went out with him several more times than I should've. I tried hard to talk myself into falling for him, but he had an unnerving habit of quoting back at me things I'd written (as well as some erectile issues that weren't really working for me either).

Though some of my most long-term boyfriends fell outside of what most would consider my physical "type"—tall and skinny with a deranged look in their eyes—the ones who stuck around eventually grew on me. That's not always the case though. Sometimes what might be considered by some to be a shallow objection proves to be insurmountable. Like say you like your girls on the more scrawny side—you're probably just going to get a punch if you ask her to starve herself into becoming your ideal.

One man I spoke with will only consider dating Indian women (he's white) and still another couldn't abide a lady with a bony behind. Kris, the fiftysomething-year-old sister of a friend of mine will only date large black men, while her sister—my friend—prefers very short, hairy Jewish guys. Go figure.

Whatever it is that gets you going, if you don't get horny when you look at your honey, the odds of a happy, long-term relationship aren't in your favor. Unless the change you require is a minor one—like if you yearn for Fabio-type long locks and he's got a crew cut, well then, that could possibly work. After all, hair grows. As long as he's willing to grow it.

Jill R., a Denver-based editor, was really excited when a friend fixed her up with a "Steve McQueen type." "He was a friend of a friend of a friend," Jill explained. Though she'd never seen his photo, Jill and Steve Jr. made plans to meet at a local bookstore. "I went in and looked and looked, and nobody even matched the description in the least. Then this guy came up behind me and said hi." To say he wasn't a Steve McQueen type would be an understatement. "He looked like the cute little leprechaun guy from Lucky Charms!" Jill laughed. "We had talked about going to dinner, but I made something up." But she was curious as to how this guy rationalized describing himself as something he so obviously wasn't. His answer: "I've got the really blue eyes and the attitude."

Check, please!

How Not to Write a Personal Ad

While having a flattering photo is—by far—the most important element of your computer-generated plea for love, you will occasionally stumble across the rare dater who actually *reads* your entire ad. The types who wade through all those troublesome words are also generally the types who won't be swayed by your pretty face and twelve-pack abs if you come off like a buffoon otherwise. So be careful. Here are a few ground rules for what not to share:

• **DO NOT MENTION YOUR MEDS INTAKE.** While many of us take SSRIs or other varieties of happy pills, that's info that's better shared on a need-to-know basis.

• **DO NOT POST A PHOTO OF YOU AND SOMEONE ELSE.** Unless it's you and someone famous, like Star Jones. If the other person is of the gender you're seeking, your audience is going to assume they're your ex—or worse, the person you're attempting to cheat on. Especially egregious are the folks who post photos taken with small children. Oh, and the same goes for pets—a transparent bid to appear sensitive, which makes all but the most dim-witted suspicious.

• **SAVE THE WHOPPERS FOR BURGER KING.** Everyone lies a little bit, but do you really think he isn't going to notice that you weigh 70 pounds more than you said you did? Ditto you guys who claim to be 6′ when you're barely 5′6″.

• DO NOT GAS ON ABOUT HOW EMBARRASSED YOU ARE TO BE TRAWLING THE PERSONALS. Who do you think you're talking to?

• DO NOT USE WORDS WHOSE DEFINITION YOU ARE LESS THAN 100 PERCENT SURE OF. Example: Desiring a "monogamous" relationship is very different than looking for a "monotonous" relationship. Though oftentimes one becomes the other.

• DO NOT LIST THE MYRIAD THINGS YOU ARE NOT LOOKING FOR. Even a skinny girl is going to get annoyed by a "no fatties" caveat. Despite the premise of this book, in this case, it's better to be positive.

• DO NOT LIST ALL THE THINGS YOU'RE NOT. "Not like other guys"? "Not high maintenance"? "Not into games"? What kind of game-playing, high-maintenance sociopath is going to admit it? None of the creeps I dated ever copped to it in advance.

• DO NOT MENTION YOUR "BITCH" OR "PSYCHO" EX. If you can't forget about them long enough to compose a personal ad, you have no business dating.

WHAT YOU HAVE TO LOOK FORWARD TO

You like Sarah Jessica Parker types; she's more Beyoncé. Or maybe your taste runs more toward tall, and you could use him as an armrest. While you should definitely be attracted to your date, sometimes love, like the exotic and foul-smelling durian fruit, takes a little time to grow on you. My friend Travis swore up and down that he could never fall in love with anyone who wasn't a natural redhead, only to end up falling in love with—and marrying—a beautiful, Brazilian brunette. So you never know . . .

PAINFULLY SHY

I had just broken up with the smelly boyfriend I mentioned earlier, when I decided to give online dating a try for the first time. Actually, if you want to get technical about it, I'd been browsing dating sites for months. Though I held off actually joining any, whenever we'd fight—which was often—I'd log on and see who I *should* have been dating instead of him. As our relationship devolved into a seemingly never-ending series of stupid arguments and passive-aggressive pouting bouts, I selected my first target and finally dumped my boyfriend by pouring an entire pint of beer over his head in front of a bunch of our friends. In case you're wondering, he deserved it.

The photo that sucked me in—and let's face it, online dating is 99 percent about looks—was of a tall, skinny, handsome guy, grinning maniacally in front of a wall of skulls—the catacombs of Paris. I should note that pretty much all my friends found this photo creepy and not at all charming, but I've never been one to pay much attention to good advice.

Paul's ad said he was a bike messenger, which at my age should've been a strike against him, but I'd just broken up with a video store clerk who smelled like rotting cheese, so it's not like I had terribly high standards in the go-getter department. Besides, he was hot.

Much to my surprise, the bike messenger—Paul— e-mailed back almost immediately upon hearing from me. He actually seemed excited that I'd written. We were going to fall in love! I'd convince him to quit pedaling around

Manhattan and get a real job! We'd move to the Upper West Side and adopt some doggies!

As much as the prospect of dating thrilled me, it also scared the crap out of me. After a year with Señor Stinky, who had been preceded by an abusive closet case, my confidence was not exactly at an all-time high. Until I agreed to meet Paul in person, I didn't realize how pathetic I'd become.

Butterflies in the tummy are kind of a cute pre-date condition. What I was suffering that day was more along the lines of vultures careening around my intestines. I stood outside the Central Park Zoo clutching my midsection, the cramping reaching its peak when the guy from the picture walked up and extended his hand.

A little bit of vomit worked its way up and into my throat by way of hello. For the next three hours I stared at him like a fool, interjecting only to meekly eke out the occasional question. Lucky for me, Paul liked to talk, so he didn't seem to notice my silence. Me, I was having trouble reconciling the bawdy fun-haver I'd always thought of myself as with this mute jackass nodding along stupidly in the middle of the Central Park Zoo.

Anne G. seems to have dated my male equivalent. "He was so shy, nervous, and self-deprecating, that he kept calling me Amy instead of Anne," she gasped. "And he was putting himself down so hard I had to tell him to quit it numerous times." To make matters even more indecipherable, "He kept talking with his hand over his mouth so I had no idea what he was saying."

Twenty-six-year-old Genevive, a Philadelphia gallery owner, had the same problem with a mumbler who was too shy to even look her in the eye. But she came up with an ingenious plan for dealing with it: "I just pretended I knew what he was saying," she laughed.

WHAT YOU HAVE TO LOOK FORWARD TO

Though we went out a bunch more times, through no fault of his, I never did feel like I could be myself around Paul. Not surprisingly, he found other, presumably more chatty girls to date. Anne's and Genevive's dates never really amounted to much either, so the message here is clear: Paralyzed by fear is a crappy way to go through life and not much fun to date either.

THE CHEAPSKATE, LEVEL I

Just below being a homicidal maniac on the no-call list resides the cheapskate, so you may be surprised to note that I've divided the cheapskate category into different levels, spread out throughout the book.

The why of it is simple, as not all cheapskates are created equal. Level I penny-pinchers are the kind of skinflints you can possibly excuse and/or train to be magnanimous contributors at some point in their lives.

These fairly harmless tightwads are generally the very young and/or extremely broke. They don't know—nor can they afford—better.

My first date was with a young man named Gary. I was about 16 and totally smitten, and my ardor only increased when he pulled up to get me in his daddy's brand-new Porsche.

I climbed in, doing my best to ignore my mom's watchful eye at the front window.

"Hi Gary," I said in the flirtiest tone I could manage. Gary looked over and grinned. "The gas gauge is on empty— let's see if we can get through the whole night without stopping for gas!" he declared.

What? I'd been so excited to ride around in a car that was guaranteed not to break down (unlike my dad's collection of clunkers), and now we were living the lyrics of some trite Jackson Browne song. Too shy to say anything, I kept my worries to myself. I was on my first date and I was going to make the best of it. Besides, it's not like I'd never been stuck on the side of the road before.

Much to my surprise, we made it to the restaurant. The owner greeted Gary like they were old buds. This is going to be fun. The man pulled my seat out for me—fancy!—and I sat down and opened the menu.

"Don't order anything too expensive," Gary instructed. I closed my menu and wondered when the fun was going to start. "I'll just have a Coke," I muttered, as Gary ordered himself a nice bowl of ravioli. I sat and mournfully sipped on my beverage as my date scarfed down his dinner. After "dinner" Gary took me to the movies—and paid—but my hopes were about as low as my blood sugar by this point. We slid into our seats, and Gary shot me the same smile I'd fallen in like with. The lights went down, and his left hand went straight to my right knee, where it remained for the remainder of the movie, rhythmically squeezing in five-second intervals. He never tried to move his hand further up my leg, nor did he try to kiss me. As the end credits rolled, he removed his hand and motioned that we should leave.

We made it home on fumes, and I never heard from him again.

WHAT YOU HAVE TO LOOK FORWARD TO

Gary was a kid, so I can't hold his miserly ways against him. In fact, I just googled him and discovered he's married, so I'm betting he probably loosened the grip on his wallet at some point in time. If this behavior is nipped in the bud at an early age, it may not prove fatal.

THE CRAZY, LEVEL I

Just as all cheapskates are not created equal, neither are all crazies.

Level I crazies can be fairly harmless—these are the types you see singing karaoke on the street or trying out for *America's Next Top Model* even though they're fat and over 40. They may annoy you, but they probably won't try to maim you.

Meet Rich G. You're going to see a lot of him pretty much anywhere crazy is mentioned in this book. North Carolinian Rich is a kind, funny, handsome single dad who has the worst luck with women of anyone I know. And that's saying something!

One day Rich and his latest prospect made a plan to go to the movies. "On the way up one of the many escalators we had to take to reach our theater, she turned to me and complained that I was 'smelling her hair.'"

"Were you?" I asked.

"NO!" he yelped. "Then she looked at the people behind and below me and loudly declared, 'What kind of person smells someone's hair on the escalator?' as if it was quite the joke. Only she was serious!

"All throughout the movie she kept asking me why I smelled her hair and assuring me it was OK that I did, and I should just admit it," he said in an incredulous tone.

"Did you go out with her again?" I inquired.

"No—movie over, date over, relationship over," he replied firmly.

Nothing wrong with a little hair sniffing!

WHAT YOU HAVE TO LOOK FORWARD TO

There are idiosyncrasies and then there's crazy. Quirky can be charming, but if you find yourself getting angry, embarrassed, or, worse, frightened by your date's behavior, you're probably dealing with the latter. In which case you should look into getting yourself a new phone number, as even the minor-league nuts can be difficult to shake.

HOW TO EXTRICATE YOURSELF

Since these dates usually occur before anyone's made too big an investment, it's fairly easy to put the kibosh on any talk of continued involvement. Sometimes a simple "Nice meeting you" upon parting will suffice because neither of you is interested in pursuing the situation.

Other times you have to be the rejecter, which, while not fun, is certainly more pleasant than being the rejectee.

As we know, Miss Karma is a bitchy little broad, so be nice about it. In other words, decline quickly and gracefully, and for fuck's sake, don't bring up her paddle-shaped thumbs or his massive, pear-shaped bottom.

PART TWO

ONE EYEBROW RAISED

THREAT LEVEL: GERANIUM

He works in pizza delivery, which just answers all your prayers, doesn't it? Man, motorbike, has own food!

—JANE, *COUPLING*

PART TWO: ONE EYEBROW RAISED

THREAT LEVEL: GERANIUM

Threat level Geranium is where things begin to escalate. There you are out on a date, innocently exchanging doe eyes at the malt shop, and suddenly something shifts. What was once a pleasant evening begins to take that familiar downward slide. Make no mistake: What we're talking about won't be pleasant, but it will be less painful than, say, a meteor slamming into your head.

Just like a Boy Scout, the experienced dater should always be prepared for the less-than-perfect outing. If that means arranging for a friend to give you a feigned emergency call at an agreed-upon time (done it) or tucking away note cards with lists of conversation topics (ditto) or always having on hand a tin of Altoids for a less-than-fresh-breathed companion, it's all part of the game. Besides, if you didn't have a crap date every now and again, you'd have nothing to measure the fantastical, magical ones against. Not only that, but the experienced dater knows how to make the most out of even the most daunting situation. Suppose it's apparent upon meeting that there is absolutely no chance of anything even remotely romantic ever developing between the two of you. It happens. Yet etiquette dictates the sporting thing to do is stick it out.

If the Buddha had written a dating mantra, I'm betting it would be "It's only an hour/don't let it suck." Sure, your date might be wearing high-waisted dad jeans or possess a distracting tic, but that's hardly Abu Ghraib–level torture. I'm not saying you should expect the worst, but there's no reason you shouldn't be ready for it if it happens. So come prepared with tickets to the circus or a big bottle of gin and try to have fun. Just kidding about the gin—excessive alcohol intake could lead to naked high jinks with an inappropriate stranger, that is, your ill-fated date.

The varieties of suitors I've listed below straddle that gray line between kinda boring and downright miserable. See if you recognize any of these types—or better yet, look deep inside yourself and see if you've ever been that guy (or girl). Surely even a charmer such as yourself has been a bad date once or twice in your life.

RUDE BOY (OR GIRL), OR SAY IT, DON'T SPRAY IT: ADVENTURES IN BAD MANNERS

My friend Claudia has the most impeccable manners of anyone I know. You never would've guessed this if you'd seen her back in college, when the two of us were marauding punk rock chicks, swigging beer that came in cans and banging boys who wore more makeup than we did. Each morning before class, Claudia would meticulously fashion her dyed black hair into foot-high spikes and powder her face until she achieved the perfect corpselike pallor. It always surprised the other students who sat with us in the cafeteria that this Gothra-like creature not only knew which fork to use at any given time, but also she never spoke with her mouth full and always had her napkin folded primly across her bondage-pantsed lap.

Though times have changed and now she's a bigtime reporter type with a tastefully (and professionally) styled chestnut 'do, Claudia's still a stickler for a well-mannered gent.

"When I was growing up I used to lose my mind because my very proper New England mother insisted on drilling us all on table manners," she told me. "Later, I was glad she did, but in a dating scenario, it's a complete curse. I have rejected two guys because they licked their knives at the table. I have to force myself to look away if anyone butters their bread before breaking it into small pieces. God forbid they take the butter directly from the dish, without first putting it on their bread plate. The slurping of soup ends any prospects for sex, and sweet Jesus, do not use the stirrer in your drink for a straw. It's a stirrer, you big pussy. Learn some manners."

I think back on all the times I've buttered my bread before breaking it into pieces and am somewhat comforted knowing that *that* must be the reason so many men opted out of calling me after our first date. Who knew?!?

Most daters I spoke with didn't have such stringent etiquette requirements, but the little things do matter. Nose-and/or butt-pickers were both cited as must-avoids, as were people who blow their nose at the dinner table—an extra ten demerits if they used the restaurant's cloth napkin. "I think at this point in life I would not go on a second date with anyone who was rude to the waitstaff or was a crappy tipper," said one fed-up lass. She added, "Life has taught me that these guys are jerks in other ways too."

Speaking of jerks, "I was out with my boyfriend and another couple that I didn't know too well," still another pal told me. "We were all getting along until then some other man they both knew stops by our table, and they proceed to talk for about ten minutes," never bothering to introduce the visitor to either of the women.

Maybe this guy's behavior seems like no biggie, which it would be if he weren't the kind of guy who referred to himself as a "feminist" and constantly talked up all the good, charitable works he performed. That is, as my friend eventually found out, when he wasn't too busy ordering up hookers off of Craigslist.

An important lesson learned: Sometimes a slurped bowl of soup can be a harbinger of other, less savory, shortcomings.

WHAT YOU HAVE TO LOOK FORWARD TO

If you're Claudia, the answer is not much, because she'll dump your ass if you dare stir your tea with a butter knife. For the rest of us, there's always the haphazardly thumbed-through copy of Emily Post—"Did you know you're not supposed to pick your teeth with your fork?!?"—or the gentle recrimination—"The manner in which you snarfed down those chili-cheese fries made me physically ill." Nobody's perfect; it's up to you to decide if you can live with someone who has no idea which fork to use.

DATING ON THE WRONG TEAM

Robert was a dead ringer for Henry Rollins, except bigger, taller, cuter, and in possession of a sense of humor. Sadly for me and my neglected lady parts, Robert liked boys. Once we got that, er, straight between us, we became fast friends.

Robert knew his sexual preference and advertised it to the world. The gay dates I'm talking about are the kind of guy who hasn't fully come to terms with the fact that he's more a sister than a mister. Let's call them the McGreeveys. Unless you are uninterested in sex, dating a gay man is an express ticket to disappointment and heartache for the straight girl. Not all gay men dating straight women are closeted—some are just oblivious. Or hopeful, reckoning that the love of a good woman will set them straight.

Defrocked reverend Ted Haggard should be able to tell you how well that works out.

Despite having what I consider a rather well-honed gaydar, I've gone out with my share of closet cases.

The first was a fun-haver I met at the local punk rock bar. The thing with Bobby was, he never informed me we were dating. I had assumed—correctly, it turned out—that he was gay and we were pals who occasionally indulged in giggly makeouts. Yet when his foxy straight friend tried to get my number, Bobby turned ten kinds of jealous. My pal Sarah had "dated" Bobby under similar circumstances the year before I did. Neither of us even got a booby feel off him, and he eventually figured out who he was. As he was always hilarious and kind, nobody ended up getting hurt.

Saffy, a 22-year-old student from Wales, found her conflicted fella online. "He was wearing a very nicely pressed shirt and designer jeans. He smoked cigarettes that came in a pastel-colored pack." While plenty of breeder boys are fastidious dressers (see also: *Seinfeld*), and there are probably nine or ten who also smoke pink ciggies, Saffy just knew. "The whole evening was very camp," she assured me.

How Not to Date a Musician in an Indie Band

Dave Burton: Tour manager of dozens of different bands you've definitely heard of

Say a lady were interested in dating (cough) someone in an indie band—what would be the exact WRONG thing to say?
"Hey, I really like your band" or "Do you like Starlite Desperation?"

Is it better to come off as a fan or feign ignorance of who they are?
Feign ignorance. The only bigger megalomaniacs than musicians are professional athletes and cock-grabbing drunken Republican politicians.

What are some of the more horrifying methods you've seen employed by groupies trying to get with band members?
Pretend passing out in the VIP area hoping for some mouth to mouth, using last week's backstage pass to sneak in, following band members up elevators in hotels, hiding in bushes and bum-rushing the tour bus door, pretending to be a journalist, offering to blow the tour manager, boasting of their intentions on band's MySpace page . . .

Does it ever help to blow the roadie?
It certainly helps the roadie. Everyone knows that roadies get more ass than musicians. What do you think is going on behind the bass cabinet during the Creedence medley in the encore?

What about showing your tits?
This only seems to happen with po-faced lesbians when there are chicks in the band. Or in Sweden.

What is the best way to get kicked off the tour bus?
Come on my bus uninvited and you are off quicker than a prom dress.

Is it better to know all the words or know none at all?
Better to mumble through your own interpretation—it's usually more poignant.

Does signing to major label change the dating/mating habits of band members? If so, how?
Absolutely. Yesterday's fuck is tomorrow's restraining order.

Dating the confused and/or in denial is not always so innocuous though. One particularly conflicted man I saw for a couple months never wanted to have sex. Blow jobs were fine (aren't they always?), and he'd slip a perfunctory finger in me now and again, but he'd never go the whole nine. God forbid he put his face down there! When I pressed him for a "why" he first told me he only liked Kate Moss types (which I'm not) and then snippily admitted that he found female genitalia "repulsive." Yet when I sensibly suggested that if that were the case, he might try dating gentlemen, he flew into a rage. Like the Reverend Haggard, he thought of himself as deeply religious, which translated to deeply in denial. I can only hope that my ex finds some inner peace and is dating a nice fella instead of doing rails off some rent boy's pecker.

WHAT YOU HAVE TO LOOK FORWARD TO

A complete lack of sex, which believe you me, will quickly prove disastrous to your self-esteem. My friend Joe had a closeted friend from college who went ahead and married a female classmate who was madly in love with him. Of course the guy wouldn't pork her, and instead of being honest, he told her he wouldn't have sex with her because she was "too fat." "Too female" is more like it. Joe was both saddened and appalled when he saw a list of goals tacked over her desk during a visit. Number one on the list: "Lose weight so [her husband] will make love to me."

THE OVERSHARER

I am divorced and my wife is a bitch. I hate her and sometimes I get so angry I lose control. But I am in theerapy [sic] and take medication. I am much better." Thus went the first line of a note I received from one date-seeking gentleman on Nerve.com.

Now normally when I got a note from someone I had no plans to go out with, I just hit "delete" and forgot about it. But I felt sorry for this guy. He was quite possibly the most clueless man I'd ever come in contact with, cyber or otherwise, and some part of me (the stupid part, no doubt) wanted to help. Against my better judgment, I wrote him back and told him that while I didn't think we were a good match for many reasons, he might want to wait until the third date or so to bring up the fact that he hated his ex-wife and was on psychiatric meds. Instead of being *grateful* for my candor and good advice, the nutter wrote back arguing that we were indeed perfect for each other and insisted we meet. Delete.

The gentleman I described above is a classic oversharer. The type who spills highly personal, sometimes highly inappropriate information to people they barely know, under the misguided notion that they're somehow being more open or honest than your average bear.

Claudia, the 40-year-old reporter we met in the bad manners section, had a more enjoyable encounter with an oversharer. Oddly enough, she also met hers—a grad student in theology—through Nerve.com, in her adopted hometown of Washington, D.C. "He was great and easy to talk to," Claudia told me over cocktails. "Dark hair and eyes . . . he was very smart, charming, unassuming. He had a strong sense of morality but was not moralistic—more of an ethical streak, informed by his theological studies." Claudia had done the unthinkable and invited him over to her apartment for their first date. (Warning: Do not attempt this at home. Claudia is a professional stunt dater. You could be maimed or worse.)

"After awhile, we started talking about relationships, and he breezily mentioned having 'blown a few guys.'"

Wait a minute. Hold the phone—shouldn't this be listed under Dating on the Wrong Team?

"Nope," Claudia elaborated, demurely sipping a glass of Shiraz. "He explained that a few guys had blown him back in school, and he felt it was the polite thing to reciprocate. So, he'd blown a few guys. I never caught a whiff of any gayness from him, which certainly challenged my belief that straight guys who 'blow a few guys' are just gays in transition." Interesting. Not really appropriate first-date chatter, but then there's nothing remotely appropriate about inviting a man you've never met into your home either. Whore!

Kidding.

The date eventually proved illuminating for Claudia and fun for her pal. "We didn't sleep together that night," she continues. "I did blow him, though. Call it a competitive streak."

Thirty-six-year-old, LA-based film executive Rose had a less fulfilling night out with an oversharer. "A friend of mine got sick of me dating struggling actors," she laughs. To aid her in breaking this streak, Rose's pal fixed her up with an old college classmate of her husband's, promising that the man in question had a stable job and no known communicable disease. It's the little things that mean so much to a lady.

"So he comes to get me and he's really good looking!" If you've ever been fixed up, you'll know why this revelation warrants an exclamation mark. "We go to the Dresden Room, which is a cool, old-school LA bar. I'm midsip in a cocktail and he says to me, 'I have really small hands and really small feet and you know what that means.'"

Incredibly, sweet naive Rose didn't. "He wouldn't stop talking about it, so I made him hold his hands up to mine. And his fingertips go up to my second knuckle! Then I asked him his shoe size. It was a size seven! But he was 6'1"! How did he walk without falling over?" Rose was puzzled but willing to deal with the tiny digits and tootsies if they came attached to a handsome guy with a job. "But he wouldn't stop bringing it up and never explained why he kept bringing it up."

The next day, Rose decided to get an outside opinion and made a quick phone survey. "My friend Fran, who's 85, explained 'it means he's got no dick!'" I suppose you could say that he was trying to warn her, but announcing your shortcomings when there's no guarantee they'll ever be found out is just foolish. Rose never returned his calls, and it wasn't because of his presumably teeny ween, but more his preoccupation with said body part.

Though you wouldn't know it by the two examples I just cited, ten-plus years of informal anthropological observations reveal that women are approximately ten times more likely to overshare than men. Probably in no small part because we tend to talk more in general. I can't even count how many times I've been seated in a restaurant, next to an obvious first date, only to cringe in horror as I listen to the female half of the couple gas on about everything from the eating disorder she suffered in the seventh grade to last month's herpes scare.

Peter M., a 52-year-old musician from Massachusetts, found his oversharer on JDate. "She went on at length—actually, it was her main topic of conversation—about the fibroid growths in her vagina," Peter told me, sounding more weary than skeeved. "This was at a New Jersey diner. And she had a really loud voice." Needless to say, Peter wasn't moved to investigate the growths himself.

WHAT YOU HAVE TO LOOK FORWARD TO

There are no secrets when you date an oversharer. You can bet on her mom and ten of her closest girlfriends being fully informed on everything from your penchant for anal to the effect that your lactose intolerance has on your intestinal tract. On the bright side, these open-book types are rarely capable of the lip-zipping it requires to be a cheater.

THE IDIOT

There's no nice way to say it, but some people are just too dumb to date. They should remain sequestered in a nice, calm environment filled with soft-angled furniture (to keep them from bruising when they inevitably bang into it) and those big squishy bats shrinks give to warring couples to help them work out their issues. This way, when they piss each other off, as they inevitably will, nobody will get hurt.

I'm not talking about people who don't know "your" from "you're"—though a certain clenched-sphincter type, ahem, might also find that supremely irritating—but the type of man or woman who seems to find exactly the wrong thing to say at the most inopportune moment possible.

Like, here's something not to do: Dan was a NYC DJ I briefly dated until he blind-cc'ed me on a saucy e-mail intended for another woman. Thinking that hearing about his and her previous night's naughtiness might turn me on (huh?!), he detailed a sex dream he'd had about her after she'd left his apartment that morning, which culminated with him dumping a load into a "tissue cunt." Though this was a dubious tactic from jump, the kicker was that he'd also included how he'd spent the prior Saturday, when he was *supposed* to have been out with me but had canceled, claiming he was tired. Judging from the activities described in his ill-advised little missive, I have no doubt he was left quite spent.

Norm D., a 36-year-old journalist from D.C., described via e-mail an exchange he had with a young lady who became confused when he mentioned a favorite author of his:

Date: What's a Nabokov?
Norm: Well, it's more of a who. Russian émigré
writer. Pretty famous . . .
Date: Anything I've read?
Norm: Uh, well, Lolita?
Date: Doesn't ring a bell.

Though this nipped any hope of romance for Norm, the pain wasn't quite over. "It ended when she shouted 'Huuuuug!' and grabbed me in the parking lot." Sweet.

In her defense, at least Norm's date wasn't deluded or pretentious. Writer/ex–*Real World* cast member Dan Renzi

What Not to Talk About

The fine art of conversation is one that many attempt, but few master. One little book isn't going to turn a rambling bore into a sparkling chatterbox, but I can help you avoid a few topics that are well-documented date doomers:

• **MARRIAGE.** Past marriages, friends' marriages, future marriages—it doesn't matter. Unless you want to either scare the crap out of your date, or, alternately, start building false hopes, the topic of weddings and what comes after should be avoided at all costs for at least the first 213 dates.

• **PROCREATION.** If you have a child at home, you need to tell the person you're out with about it (which is only fair), so go for it. Otherwise, for the same reasons you avoid talking about weddings, it's best to avoid baby talk.

• **BAD HABITS.** Let your new special friend get to know you a little before confessing your fondness for illicit substances and tranny hookers.

• **TRAUMATIC EVENTS FROM YOUR PAST.** I'm struggling for a sensitive way to say this, but telling someone you barely know that your past includes episodes that would make Jerry Springer cry is a good way to scare off a nice person or alert a bad person that you'll be an easy mark. Do not wear your heart, or your history, on your sleeve.

- **EXES.** If he/she/it was such an unrepentant jackass, what does that make you for dating him/her/it?

- **PRENUPS.** Now why on earth would anyone bring up their position on prenups (pro, naturally) on a second date? I never did find out, because I refused to go out on a third.

- **YOUR SELF-HELP LIBRARY.** I knew a lady who went home with someone only to discover that the sole book on her date's shelf was *The Secret*. Guess who didn't get laid? I don't care if it's *The Game* or *Men Who Hate Women and the Women Who Love Them*—someone you're thinking about schtupping doesn't need to know that you purchase your therapy at Barnes & Noble.

- **ICKY MEDICAL CONDITIONS.** Ideally, you want your paramour to picture you naked, not covered in weeping sores.

- **SEXUAL FANTASIES.** Unless your date has segued smoothly into naked and sweaty, there's no reason to share your predilection for light bondage and anal beads. That's definitely third-date material.

found himself with possibly the worst kind of dolt—the kind who pretends to be smart:

This guy—beautiful, beautiful guy, made my knees shake—calls me a few days after we met in a bar. He asked, "What are you doing?" I said, "I'm cleaning my apartment." He asked, "When can you be ready to go?" I said in an hour. He replied, "I'll be there in 30 minutes," and hung up. Sexy, right? Love the cocky thing like that.

Well. He picks me up, and we go to the Metropolitan Museum of Art to see a Salvador Dali show. We walked around, looked at the art—everything was great.

Then we wandered into the permanent exhibitions, and suddenly he knew so much about all the paintings, telling me the history of each one, who painted them, all of it. He was suddenly an expert, even though in the Dali exhibit he didn't say a word.

But at one point when he walked ahead a little, I glanced at the little placard next to one of the paintings—and it said everything he told me, basically word for word! He had just memorized all the little signs! Apparently he brought a lot of dates there.

Brooklyn-based yoga instructor Betty found herself having coffee with a dum-dum who had delusions of grandeur. "I met up with this geeky guy, which was fine, until he proceeded to talk about fat chicks. For an *hour*." Though she's quite lean, Betty found the topic distasteful and tried to change the subject, bringing up some Greek mythology she'd been reading. "He managed to segue into it, à la: 'It's not Zeus's fault for turning himself into various animals and cheating on Hera—if Hera hadn't been drinking so much ambrosia and getting fat . . .'"

Bay Area filmmaker Karen I. laughingly told me about one incident where she was the moron. "It was an Internet date," she shared. "I lied about my age, saying that I was 40, but I was really 45." As we discussed earlier, this is definitely an error in judgment, but no biggie. Unfortunately, that wasn't the extent of her boo-boo. "We were having wine at my place, and I had been on a television show that he expressed interest in seeing." Karen put the tape in the VCR. "The host of the show asked my age, and I responded with '45.' He was, of course, shocked, since he was 36."

Confessions of a Reformed Leg Humper

I never look at women as whores if they give me sex on the first date. In fact, I prefer it. But when I was younger, I had a three-date rule: If, after three dates, it didn't look like there was going to be sex, I'd just go.

So I took this girl to see that Prince movie Graffiti Bridge *and immediately started hounding her for sex.*

She goes, "I don't think we know each other well enough." And I told her, "This is the third date; if we don't have sex tonight, I'm never going to call you again."

—DAVID, 40, WRITER

OK, it's getting worse, but Karen hadn't quite finished alienating her younger man. "A bit later in the date, I got a call on my cell phone—never answer your phone during a date," she warned. "It was a famous guy who I had met the week before, and my cell phone was on speaker, but I didn't realize it until it was too late."

Uh-oh. "The famous dude said, 'You gave me the best head I've ever had—I only lasted about forty-five seconds!'

My date heard the whole thing." Gulp. "I turned to the guy and said, 'I bet I never see *you* again, ha ha.'" Well, at least she got that part right.

WHAT YOU HAVE TO LOOK FORWARD TO

- A sore hand from smacking yourself upside the head

- Deep, red-faced embarrassment if you run into any of your friends while out with this person

- Wrinkles caused by incessant frowns of bewilderment

- A precipitous drop in your own IQ, as it's a fact that stupid is a highly contagious condition

THE MOPE

I don't even know why I bother anymore," my Nerve.com date blurted by way of hello, looking me up and down with a look of disappointment he didn't even bother to finesse.

"Hi, I'm Judy," I offered perkily, extending my hand for a hello shake.

Señor Mope reluctantly gave me a half-hearted hand jiggle and motioned for me to sit. I slid onto the barstool, ordered a drink, and took a stab at a chat. He kept eyeing me with the same doleful expression, offering only shrugs and monosyllabic grunts in reply. Talking to him was like throwing words into a vortex. Stuff went in and nothing came out. I would've left, except I have a firm policy about abandoning perfectly nice cocktails.

I eventually managed to draw him out a little bit, and it turned out that it wasn't *me* specifically Marty Mope was disappointed in, just the business of dating in general. When he saw me, he correctly assumed that we wouldn't be a match. But while *he* thought we didn't match for what-ever reason—who cares?—I knew we weren't going to hit it off because I'd made an oath that I'd never again date the clinically depressed (unless they were well medicated).

Alek was another sad sack. A friend of a friend, this smart, good-looking guy couldn't figure out why he couldn't find a girlfriend. The night we met—*not* on a date, but just a friendly outing with mutual pals—he found out I was an advice columnist and took the opportunity to lament his sad state of affairs. "My girlfriend dumped me," he moaned, in a thick Russian accent. I nodded in commiseration. Getting dumped sucks. It's a feeling I'm quite familiar with.

"I'll never love anyone like I loved her. She was perfect," he went on. "There is no love left in the world. She was my one true love."

OK, right there, he lost me. I don't know about you, but I think there's possibly no bigger ass-chapper than someone who claims they've lost their mythical "one." I happen to know for a fact that there are at least fifty—probably hundreds more—"ones" for any given person. And I've found it's inevitable that the brand of whiner who clings to this notion is the one who annoyed their partner—oh, sorry, "the one"—into leaving in the first place.

But I was trying to be nice, so I suggested he give a woman he worked with a shot. He had been talking about how smart and nice she seemed. "Is wrong to date where you work," Alek replied mournfully. There's a certain school of thought that believes this to be true, so I took a look at the book he was carrying around with him and suggested a book club. He looked at me like I'd sprouted tentacles. Sigh. "How about online dating?" I asked, pointing out that it'd worked for me. "I tried it once and it was terrible. The girls I like don't like me; the girls who like me, I don't like . . ."

Trying online dating *once* is like eating one potato chip. You need to eat at least half a bag to get any satisfaction. And if you can slather it in onion dip, all the better. The fact is, Alek didn't really want a girlfriend. He wanted an audience for his misery. No wonder his ex gave him the heave-ho—I was ready to slit my wrists after spending fifteen minutes with his mopey ass.

WHAT YOU HAVE TO LOOK FORWARD TO

You know how I said earlier that stupid was contagious? That was a lie. Depression really is, though. Seriously. Just try to remain chipper hanging out with a partner who not only sees the glass as half empty, but suspects that the liquid bit is filled with a toxic concoction.

And while yes, depression is a serious condition, it is also very treatable. The people I'm talking about here aren't willing and/or interested in helping themselves. And these types always want to bring you along for the ride. That whole "misery loves company" myth—not such a myth.

WOULD YOU LIKE SOME CRACKERS WITH YOUR CHEESE?

I don't know about you, but dinner out at a restaurant with my dad means a lot of time spent wanting to crawl under the table as he "jokes" with the waitress. Answering, "It's great—you're a really good cook!" after she's dutifully inquired as to how we're doing is his idea of high hilarity. He either doesn't notice or doesn't care that he's the only one laughing. Dating the cheeseball is a lot like dating your dad—albeit without the nasty incestuous connotations.

Dan Renzi's aforementioned museum date was one such *fromage* aficionado. "He told me how beautiful I was when I stood there looking at the art; the way my body curved with my weight on one leg . . . so graceful . . . and then he told me, 'Your eyes are the color of the ocean.'" Instead of being moved to, say, fellate his date, Dan nearly doubled over laughing and demanded the unimaginative guy say it again. "I said, 'Thank you! I really am!' I couldn't stop laughing. He brought me home and never spoke to me again."

I can't say I really blame the dude for being insulted, but I don't handle compliments—insincere or otherwise—very well either. But compliments offered only because the giver is trying to talk their way into the sack are just downright insulting. I remember being out with this hedge fund something-or-other one night, and even though I had a really bad cold with all the requisite dripping and chapping—as well as a *gigantic*, bright red cold sore covering half my upper lip—the Hedgehog would not stop gassing on about how hot I was. There's no false modesty at work here—I looked like crap (and infectious crap at that!). In fact, at one point I even checked in the bathroom to see if my looks had magically improved since leaving the house, but nope.

WHAT YOU HAVE TO LOOK FORWARD TO

The news isn't all bad. If you can endure the daily embarrassments these people will subject you to and fool yourself into believing that the lies they're shoveling is the truth, I predict holidays loaded with teddy bears bearing heart-shaped pillows. Valentine's Day will no longer be spent scarfing frosting straight from the can but instead marked with Mylar balloons embossed with sentimental sayings ("I

Wuv U!") and underpants that have been intricately folded into little floral shapes. Things could be worse. You could be smitten with . . .

THE BAD KISSER!

Nothing is as exciting and/or as frightening as the first kiss. The nervousness, the anticipation, the sometime scariness of it all! After all, the first kiss sets the tone for the entire relationship—or helps determine if indeed there will *be* a relationship.

If there were advanced degrees in dating, I'd have a triple PhD by now, so the fact that I've known a bad kisser or two in my time should come as no surprise. Starting off on the wrong foot, even my first kiss was disastrous.

Tommy wore scandalously tight blue jeans and his long stringy hair flipped back into wings. I never saw him without a big ole comb sticking out of his back pocket. Tommy also came equipped with the longest tongue this side of Gene Simmons. While I'm sure this came in handy later in life, the reality of our first kiss was less a tender moment than an act akin to having a baby's forearm jammed down your throat. Having nothing to compare it to, this trauma—my first kiss—led me to believe I didn't like kissing boys and therefore must actually be a lesbian. Sadly, this later turned out not to be the case.

Ben, the bisexual barista from the local hipster coffee shop, was another rotten kisser, albeit one I experienced much later along in life. I cooked him dinner on our second date, sure that the awkward smooching from our first date had been some kind of aberration. After telling me he had been thinking about me all day, I counted myself lucky to have found a man who actually copped to his feelings. Any worries I had about him preferring penises to pussies evaporated as he looked me up and down with a stare that spelled trouble of the most fun variety. I sauntered across the kitchen, grabbed him by the collar, and planted a moist (not a wet!) one right on his lips. He kissed me back, jaws clenched shut. I went in for a second one, this time opening my mouth a little and giving the slightest bit of tongue. Again, no entry granted. Have you ever tried to make out with someone who won't open their mouth?

On the opposite end of the bad-kissing spectrum was my ex of six years, aka quite possibly the world's worst kisser. On a quick-peck basis, he was fine. But once you started to get down to it, it was the stuff how-not-to videos are made of.

I'd be feeling all frisky and look up only to see a wide-open mouth full of expensive dental work and a fully extended tongue zooming toward me. It was frightening. And his mouth was so large that it often covered both my lips and nose, making breathing an issue.

Try as I might, I could never train him. I tried everything (except telling him he was a lousy kisser—that seemed cruel). I'd put a knuckle against each jaw hinge, slip my thumbs under his chin, and attempt to squeeze his mouth shut a little. It never worked, and I'd inevitably emerge gasping for air with a nose covered in drool.

Not all bad kissers are irredeemable though. The Lithuanian sculptor I was obsessed with for a couple years also started out as a bad kisser, of the dry, lip-locked variety. He, however, was a willing pupil, and by the time he dumped me I had transformed him into a kisser of knee-weakening dimension. I'm sure the skanky-ass Mackenzie Phillips lookalike he threw me over for enjoyed him and his great big beautiful mouth very much.

Like Jill Sobule, I've kissed a girl, and it was a lot of fun. Because we are the slightly more sensitive gender, I figured that girls were better kissers than men in general. Most of the straight men I spoke with admitted that they thought this was the case too. "A lot of times men are just twiddling their thumbs, biding their time till they get to stick their dicks in," my friend Travis concurred.

Only one woman I interviewed copped to being a problematic kisser. "Once I got so tipsy I started making out with my date's nose," 32-year-old yoga instructor Betty shared with me. In Betty's defense, she *was* liquored up, and she did realize her technique was lacking. This is in sharp contrast to the clean and sober bike messenger I dated who insisted on mid-makeout chin licking. In case you're tempted to try this at home, not hot. Not even a little.

Zack, a musician/poet in his mid-twenties, has also experienced the less-than-appealing lady lip locker (and as far as I know, he and Betty have yet to meet): "The problem is, a lot of girls just shove their tongues down your throat." Clever Zack has come up with a way to remedy the problem: "You go for the lip lock—block their tongue with your lips and maybe bite their lower lip lightly." As for setting your jaw in stone, Zack says no. "The teeth lock can be embarrassing. You only do that when you don't want to kiss them at all." He admits that even this careful course of action is not foolproof. "If you like them enough, you put up with it," he shrugged.

WHAT YOU HAVE TO LOOK FORWARD TO

You have several options when dating a bad kisser, none of them particularly fun or easy:

- You cut and run—recommended if you're not terribly enthused about the other person in the first place.

- You learn to accept that your immediate future does not include weak-knee-inducing makeouts. Take it from one who knows—this is not a fun option.

- You teach them how to be a better kisser—not always possible—but if you really like the sloppy smacker, well worth trying.

THE CHEAPSKATE, LEVEL II

Though his photo on Nerve.com was a bit blurry, I got suckered in by the cute dog Luke was roughhousing with in his ad. He told me he was a screenwriter and pursued me ardently. By this point in my online dating career, I didn't expect much but agreed to go out with him.

Warning bell number 1: He wanted to meet at an art opening, which I was fine with until he added that the reason he picked an opening was "because the drinks are free." Erm, cheap white wine isn't exactly a bank-buster, even for a marginally employed type such as myself. Didn't this guy write screenplays? Most of my screenwriter friends make a pretty good living, even if their movies rarely get made. Hmm.

Warning bell number 2: The reason his photo was blurry was because it was probably taken with the first Brownie camera. Luke was a *lot* older than the blur had led me to believe, and I never would've recognized him if he hadn't found me first.

Warning bell number 3: As he introduced himself, I could see the woman manning the wine table—a woman I'd never met—make a little grimace. I guess it was obvious that this was our first meeting, because as I watched her over his shoulder (he had his back to her), she began mouthing the word "NO!" at me, all the while waving her hands and vehemently shaking her head!

Four-alarm fire: After what I guesstimated was his seventh or eighth glass of gallery rotgut (he'd gotten there early—go figure!), he suggested we repair to a bar around the corner. We sidled up to the bar and placed our orders. I knew better than to expect him to pay, but I was not prepared for him to turn to me, as he grabbed his beer, and say "I'll get you next date." *Next date?!?*

I was too shocked to say anything and gulped my beer so I could excuse myself quickly. (Please note that people with last names like McGuire will finish their beer even under the most hostile conditions.) As I left, Luke tried to insist he'd drive me home, as payback for the beer he'd tricked me into buying him. No thanks. Unlike Luke, I had cab fare.

WHAT YOU HAVE TO LOOK FORWARD TO

Women who do what Luke did are called gold diggers. As far as I know, there's no equivalent term for men. Whether it's a man or a woman cheapskate you're dating, your situation will turn out the same—financially depleted. Unless you've got a secret closet full of hundred-dollar bills in your apartment, you will eventually find yourself as broke as your date. Not only that, but paying for everything will eventually get on your nerves, so then you'll start getting cranky, which will lead to grimacing, which leads to wrinkles, which, in turn, will cause you to consider Botox. So

How Not to Date a DJ

Kurt B. Reighley (aka DJ El Toro): KEXP, clubs,
weddings, corporate events, bar/bat mitzvahs

Okay, so you're DJing at a club and a sassy young hottie walks up and asks you to play his favorite song. What are the top five libido-killers he could request?

Britney, Madonna, Cher, a song I just played . . . or the one I'm playing right now. Trust me, that happens all the time. (For the record, Britney, Madonna and Cher have all made records I like—I just hate people who are predictable.)

Could you ever date a Celine Dion fan?

Yes, if he was from Quebec, didn't know English, bathed once a month, and simply laughed in my face when I begged him to change the music. Naturally I mean "date," not date.

What if he had a really big dick?

See above. If you're that invested in the fantasy, size is probably inconsequential.

What song, if it came on the radio when you were mid-schtup, would cause you to lose your boner?

Once I went home with a guy, and, in the middle of the deed, an Alanis Morrisette "rock block" came on the radio. I was (a) surprised to see him display a level of excitement heretofore absent from his conduct, and (b) found it very challenging to remain, um, engaged.

Clubs, bar mitzvahs, or weddings—which gathering has the most painful taste in music and why?
Weddings, no contest. Mitzvahs are for teens, so they want to hear new music, and lots of it. Weddings always require playing the same 100 tired songs, every time, even when the client has said they "don't want the same old wedding songs." You try telling the mother of the bride you won't play "Dancing Queen" after she's downed a couple glasses of bubbly.

So you're at a wedding and there's a member of the bridal party who is so cute you can't stand it. You make plans for later, but first he has to get through rest of the wedding, which means dancing. The Macarena or a Kenny Chesney–inspired country-western line dance—which is more of a boner-killer?
The Macarena. Watching middle-aged men and women slapping their butts and grinding in a circular motion is very unsettling. Line-dancing at least involves a moderate degree of dexterity.

What is the worst line anyone's ever used on you at work? Or the worst thing a guy who's hitting on you could possibly say?
The fellow who came up while Patti Labelle was playing, pointed at me, and said, "I've got a YOU attitude."

Is there an oft-requested song that you out and out refuse to play? If so, which one?
Believe it or not, no. See the following answer.

If there is one, can you be bribed into playing it? If you can, what would it take?

If I'm working a private event, I'm basically a human jukebox. I will play whatever the clients and their guests want. Tips are nice, but I charge a very "fair" fee in exchange for taking a moderate amount of abuse. If someone is insisting on something really inappropriate for the mood—like Gipsy Kings when everyone is losing their minds to Beyoncé, I will politely lie, ask them to wait awhile, and hope they drink too much to remember. If they remember? Eventually, I'll play it. Eventually.

In a club, it's amazing what a five- or ten-spot and a smile will do to change up my playlist for a few songs. The smile—sincere, not condescending—is more important than the cash, actually.

Are there any songs people request only because they think it'll impress you by making them seem cooler than they actually are?

Nobody tries to impress the DJ with knowledge. We're "the help." They try to impress us with money and attitude. Good luck.

Who's easier—musicians or DJs?

Musicians. They're all about ego. DJs are about, ahem, sharing and taste-making.

Please name your fashion deal-breaker.

Any item of apparel I can see my reflection in.

when you say no to cheapskates, what you're really doing is rejecting a future filled with injections of botulism into your face.

LIAR, LIAR, PANTS ON FIRE—ADULT SWIM

The fibs that we talked about in Part One were fairly innocuous—a few inches added, a couple pounds deleted, and five or six years subtracted. The second-tier fibber is more problematic.

Ellen L., a kinky 22-year-old NYU student, found herself intrigued with a man she met on a popular BDSM Web site:

I am a dominant. I'm not submissive at all, and this guy's profile comes up, and the first thing that catches my eye is the headline: "High School Dropout Specializing in the Domination of Highly Intelligent Women."

The profile was long and very well written . . . I thought it was weird he was a dropout yet wanted to sexually dominate these highly educated women. I wanted to learn more.

We e-mailed back and forth and didn't talk much about his profile. He told me I was the first person who ever wrote him. He said he hated the educational system and preferred to learn on his own.

I was close to graduation when this happened, and up until this point I never cared to date anyone who wasn't educated. But something about him seemed attractive. I couldn't believe he wasn't educated—I thought he must be a genius or something.

He picks me up and we go out for sushi. I meet a lot of people in this realm, and you learn pretty quick to gauge someone by the energy they give off. The first thing I figured out was that this guy was captain of the math team—no way was he dominant.

We ate dinner, went back to my place, and then he said he had something to tell me. I was sure he was going to tell me he wasn't dominant, but instead he told me that he had actually graduated college. I thought that was a pleasant surprise, but before I could say anything, he added that he was actually in law school and on scholarship and number 2 in his class!

It didn't even occur to me that this person must be really fucked up; it seemed like a good thing to find out that he was educated and wrote for the law review. I wanted to know why he made up this ridiculous story.

He claimed it was because he had always been dorky and girls never liked him, but as soon as he got into law school, women started flocking toward him. He felt like women were only interested in him because he was doing better and decided that if he made up this whole alter ego, he'd find someone who was into him for his real personality. It made sense, and I felt a little sympathy for him.

He lived on Long Island with his mother, and one night I went out to visit him—we hadn't even kissed yet. He picked me up from the train, and we went out to the beach. It was dark, the moon was full . . . everything seemed perfect. I leaned in to kiss him.

He jumped back and said, "Not now, I want to wait until the timing is perfect."

What?!? I mean, it was summer. We were on the beach—the moon, the sound of the water . . . it just doesn't get more perfect than that!

Instead we go back to his place, and because he lived with his mom, I couldn't sleep in his room. So

I'm laying in the guest room, and I hear a knock on the door—it's him standing there, completely naked.

I figure, OK. So he hops into bed and we start cuddling. We still haven't kissed, and he starts masturbating. I asked him, in the sexiest way I could muster, if he liked blow jobs.

He says, "Maybe some other time—not now!" He kept masturbating and chanting "Tell me I'm your boy, tell me I'm just your toy!" All this crazy stuff, out of nowhere. It all revolved around me being smarter than him and taking advantage of him. It was more just incredibly freaky. He had no desire for me to touch him or get physical with him. I was just a prop in his fantasy. I sent him back to his room.

Ellen took the first train out of there the next morning and never saw her young fibber again—though not for lack of trying on his part. All was not for naught though, as young Ellen learned a valuable lesson: "It taught me that if you meet someone and you find out that they've lied about everything they've told you, you shouldn't date him even if he seems like a nice guy."

WHAT YOU HAVE TO LOOK FORWARD TO

As the Thompson Twins so eloquently put it, "Lies, lies, lies, yeah, they're gonna get you!" More to the point, as Ellen's story so perfectly illustrates, hook up with a liar and not only will you not get laid, you'll have to schlep all the way out to Long Island to get rejected.

WHAT NOT TO SAY (SPECIFICALLY)

There are plenty of Web sites and books dedicated to supplying you, the reader, with pickup lines guaranteed to get you laid. These are some of the somewhat less successful lines I've collected from various sources:

- "Let's make CUDDLEBUNNIES!!!"

- "Dolly Parton's 'Jolene' was probably written about a woman just like you."

- "Your breasts are the reason I asked you out—well, that and you seem like you'll be dirty in bed."

- "Let me just put it in—I promise not to move it."

- "You remind me of my mom/dad/brother/sister."

- "Would it be rude of me to come over and bury my face in your cleavage right now?"

- "I am like a girl so you have to drive me home."

- "You are a little soft . . . you do not work out?"

- "Damn baby, you fine! I don't like dem skinny girls!"

- "I can't figure out if you're thick or if you're fat. Thick or fat: I just don't know!"

- "Can I get your sister's number?"

- "Are you sure you're a virgin? You don't feel like a virgin."

- "I have been waiting to fuck you since I saw you in a bathing suit last year." (Said by one woman's best friend who went on to become her best stalker.)

- "You have a head like the death star with a smiley face on it."

- "I can't love you, but if you are okay with that, I would still like us to sleep together."

- "I still talk to [my ex] because I want to keep both doors open."

- "If I could take your boobs and put them on her body, it would be the perfect woman."

- "If you just let me, I promise you won't get any diseases."

- "If you go on a diet and start working out, I can keep seeing you."

- "You're above average."

- "Oh yeah, I do heroin all the time. But I shoot up between my toes so that the marks don't show in photos. Do you want to see?"

BOTH EYEBROWS FURROWED IN HORROR

THREAT LEVEL: ENDIVE

The worst thing a man can ever do is kiss me on the first date.

—HALLE BERRY

PART THREE:
BOTH EYEBROWS
FURROWED IN HORROR

THREAT LEVEL: ENDIVE

Wow. Really? Ms. Berry must live in a far kinder and gentler world than mine, because where I come from, the worst thing a man can ever do has generally involved a foul-smelling bodily expulsion, lots of yelling, and possibly a felony. A kiss?!? Not to be cruel, but this from a woman who married a wife beater and then traded him in for a sex addict? Methinks Ms. Berry can come up with something better than a simple little liplock.

Welcome to the jungle. In the first half of this book we discussed simple dates gone wrong: He was too fat, she was too loud, and the like. While these dating mishaps were not what anyone would call fun, they ran just a hair too mild to be categorized as catastrophic—just your average mistakes and misconnections that anyone could find themselves guilty of after too little sleep, too many Mallomars, an unfortunate haircut, or even a low-level hangover.

Threat level Endive is where things ratchet up several dozen notches. Whereas the peeps described in the first half might've been misguided, unattractive, or a tad unpleasant, here's where things get ugly. Charm will be in short supply over the next few dozen or so pages, but where that's lacking, instead you'll find pathos, drama, intrigue, and downright nuttiness.

As you may have gathered from my encyclopedic knowledge of dates gone wrong, I've pretty much experienced firsthand just about every variety of courting catastrophe you could possibly imagine. Note that I've lived to tell the tale, and not only that, but because I've canoodled with so many loons and thus developed such a high tolerance for bad behavior, we're only now getting to the kind of date I consider irreparably awful. You probably thought we were well ensconced by Part Two.

I like to think of myself as a relatively clever, intuitive lady, yet only once or twice did I have any inkling beforehand that these rotten dates would turn out as horribly as they did. Because I work as a dating advice columnist, even when my date turned out to be a ringer for Charles Manson, I would often stick around in the name of research. But even if you're not a dating professional, I urge you to give even the rottenest of apples a couple minutes of your time. Just think of the stories you'll have for your friends. And isn't that what dating is all about?

Oh, wait . . . no, it's *not* actually, is it? Dating is *supposed* to be a series of auditions for your next great love. Ha. It'd be nice if all attempts at romance turned out like movies on the Hallmark Channel, but sometimes they're more Sci Fi, Lifetime (yikes!), or Discovery Channel.

You'll note that in the first half of the book, each variety of awful date was followed by a brief note explaining what you'd be getting yourself into if you ignored the red flags. You won't find those cute little notes in this half. If someone behaves the way these daters do, you're not allowed to see them again. Sure, you can finish your—first and *only*—cocktail, but I can't permit you to ever go out with them again ever. Never. Do you hear me?

Are you listening?

NEVER.

HI, I'M INAPPROPRIATE!

M y mom is really hot. I've always been really attracted to her. We're very close."

So said the fortysomething booking agent/party promoter/[insert nebulous career of choice here] I had agreed to go out with in a moment of monumental stupidity. I took a big swig of beer and wondered what the fuck I was doing with my life. I mean, his *mom*? And why—*why* was he telling *me* that he not-so-secretly wanted to bang the lady who'd given birth to him? Isn't that the kind of confession only a licensed therapist should be fielding? I mean, yuck.

I hadn't been attracted to Clyde from jump—which is a bad sign online, as everyone puts their best pic forward. But I was going through this whole give-a-guy-a-chance phase—which began and ended with him—and figured I'd give him a go.

From the moment he sat down, Clyde (who I suspected was wearing at least concealer, possibly mascara) had been spewing out pretty much everything that flitted through his obviously addled brain. I'd heard about how he rented his apartment out for porn shoots, how he was wrestling between labeling himself a filmmaker or merely sticking with the broader "artist" definition, but mostly about all the women in his life. Clyde confided that he was rarely attracted to women as old as I—who was still quite a few years his junior—and generally preferred much younger ladies. I can only guess I reminded him of his mother.

Sarah, a 30-year-old teacher, met her Mr. Wrong overseas. "I was teaching English in Korea, and my one-year contract was almost over," she told me via e-mail. "During my last month there I had started seeing a friend. We had already slept together at this point."

The two went to see *Bodies: The Exhibition*. "You know, the preserved cadavers and organs in plastic," she clarified. "I wasn't sure if I was amused or a little freaked out when he offered to give me five bucks if I kissed one of the bodies."

Believe it or not, *that's* not the disturbing part of this date. "Afterwards, we went to Subway because we had worked up such an appetite looking at hacked-up corpses and deformed fetuses, and over subs he told me about how his boss was trying to arrange a marriage for him with a receptionist at his dentist's office. She supposedly needed

How Not to Date a Porn Star #1

Tera Patrick: Founder of Teravision and star of countless adult films, including *Stimula*, *Aroused*, and *Fire and Ice*

You've had several different careers—what would you say is the biggest difference between the guys who hit on you when you were a nurse or fashion model and the men who hit on you today?
They're a little more aggressive when you're a porn star. They think they're going to get more out of you.

What is Tera Patrick's ultimate turn-off?
Bad hygiene and someone who's too forward.

Is there an item of clothing you believe no man should be allowed to wear?
A thong. Definitely no male thongs.

What's the worst thing a guy can say to a porn star he wants to date?
"When are we going to have a threesome?" When you're a porn star everyone assumes you're automatically into girls and you always have sex with your girlfriends. Before I was a porn star, I never had guys asking for a threesome.

Would you prefer a potential date had seen all or at least some of your movies or none at all?

None at all. That way there's no preconceived opinions about who I am and what I will or won't do. My husband hadn't seen any of my movies before we met. It's kind of funny—when my sister was dating, it was hard for her because men kept asking her if she was like her sister.

Say you went home with a guy and you found out he had all your DVDs and the Tera Patrick Perfect Pussy™. Would that be a yay or a nay?
I would definitely get up and leave.

Have you ever been a really bad date?
Yeah. I've been there. I've gotten drunk and passed out, which I guess could possibly qualify me as a good date. I've bailed on a few guys who didn't meet my requirements. I went on a date with this rugby player who was tall and muscular and he had a really small penis. I walked out on him. Size really does matter to me.

Wow. I can't believe a guy with a tiny dick had balls enough to go home with you!
Yeah, well . . .

Did your husband do anything weird or inappropriate the first time you guys went out?
Evan didn't do anything that bothered me, but he did call his ex-girlfriend thinking we were going to have a threesome. There was just no way. She was not attractive to me at all. We had a talk.

to be married in the next three months, or so said her fortune teller."

Sarah's class-act date was considering the offer but wasn't quite done pitching woo at Sarah yet. "He also complained that he couldn't afford the high-class prostitutes in Korea. I never thought he—or any other decent person— would have the audacity to talk about their fondness of prostitutes and the arranged marriage that might be happening soon with the person they're boning!"

I think the key word there is "decent." Honesty is a noble concept, but there are definitely some times when a zipped lip is the way to go.

YOUR EXIT STRATEGY

The beautiful thing about being out with someone highly inappropriate is that you can amuse yourself by making up any old reason to get out of there:

- "Ouchie—my anal warts are burning, and I left my special cream at home."

- "Can I borrow a hundred bucks?"

- "Oh God, the mescaline is starting to kick in . . . why are you wearing a frog?"

- "Guess how loud I can yell. No, really—guess!"

I LOVE YOU—WHAT WAS YOUR NAME?

Long before a straight girl sprouts her first down-there hair we learn to stifle the urge to vocalize what we are thinking—at least when we're talking to boys. Woe betide the lady who imagines out loud how cute her sofa will look in his parentally financed condo—or worse, comes out and mentions the M word. By the time we buy our first training bra, we dames know to keep this line of thinking to ourselves, because it's a fact that a woman who mentions envisioning any kind of future together on the first fifty or so dates with a man will most likely never see him again.

Not that this is necessarily such a bad thing. We ladies don't need to be getting ahead of ourselves.

Though you'd think this is a case of what's good for the goose would be good for her male counterpart, for some reason, men don't seem to be taught using the same set of rules. True, most of them are utterly uninterested in any talk of even the shakiest kind of semipermanence when it comes to relationships, yet there is a certain breed of boy who wants nothing more than to settle down and have you start pushing out babies immediately. Does it come as a shock that most of these guys are highly dysfunctional?

I've had dudes—inevitably the less attractive ones— declare themselves my boyfriend halfway through the first date and decide they were madly in love before we'd even had sex. They'd talk about marriage before we'd even found out each other's middle names. As I alluded to earlier, one guy I was seeing asked me my thoughts on prenups on our *second date*.

Still, that doesn't quite match the nuttiness of my lawyer friend Fred's one-night stand who, seconds after completing the act, began rocking back and forth, muttering "I love you, I wanna have your baby" over and over again. Did I mention that the trick was another dude?

One of Jen Dziura's men was perhaps even more presumptuous than that—at least Fred's date waited until after they'd done the deed. "He was a medical student who was a tremendous literalist, to the point that I suspected he might be mildly autistic," Jen reported. "His ability to understand subtlety, irony, sarcasm, or implication approached absolute zero."

Not only that, but Jen's date "explained very clearly that he wanted to find a life partner as soon as possible, buy a boat, retire to the Mediterranean, and have his wife have five to six of his children (which he would deliver himself) on this boat in the middle of the Mediterranean."

Ahoy, matey! While it's good to have plans and goals in life, Jen's date quickly crossed the line to creepy. Chalk it up to his extreme case of social retardation, but her gasp of horror didn't register, and onward he charged. Instead of pretending to be a normal person and maybe changing the subject, Dr. McNightmare "proceeded to ask point-blank if I would like to have children."

"I don't know," Jen answered honestly. Undeterred, her date forged ahead. "If you did have children, would you like to have five or six of them?"

Understandably, Jen informed him that that sounded like a whole lot of kids, but her hell-bent-on-procreating future husband wasn't hearing that. "How about having them on a boat?" he implored.

Jen excused herself and performed a DIY tubal ligation on the train ride home.

YOUR EXIT STRATEGY

Remember that time you got drunk and told your one-night stand you loved him? Recall what that guy said, and use it yourself:

- "Look, babe, I'm not able to handle any kind of heavy commitment right now."

- "Uh, I gotta go."

Or you could bust a political cap in his ass:

- "Marriage is a patriarchal institution that reduces women to a commodity. I want no part of it and am incensed you thought I was that kind of girl, er, woman."

While most examples in this book can be true whether you're male or female, gay or straight, as evidenced by about a million bad jokes, lesbians are exempt from this one.

POLITICALLY INCORRECT

I've never bought that line about avoiding talk of religion or politics on the first date. Yes, politics and religion cause arguments, but if I'm sitting across from Rush Limbaugh Jr., better I know sooner rather than later. Color me intolerant, but although I can handle bad breath, I am unwilling to waste even half a beer getting to know someone who believes Fred Phelps has a point.

Paul, a Nebraska-based grad student, feels the same way. "I went out with this woman who had a PhD in psychology," he told me. "She also turned out to be a Jesus freak who used the word 'fag' a lot." Paul faked an emergency phone call an hour into their magical evening. What *did* we do before cell phones?

As I'm sure is shocking to absolutely no one by this point, I've also done my time with a red stater, if only ideologically speaking. Remember the guy who mentioned the prenup? That was Larry. Not surprisingly, Larry worked in finance. Exactly what that entailed I couldn't tell you, but he was rich, and once again, I was trying to date outside my type. Because he played his leanings close to the vest, I even went out with him twice. I started to get a feeling things weren't going to work out between us when, over colorful cocktails, he told me at great length how almost every woman he'd been meeting up to that point wanted to look like Jennifer Aniston. And how refreshing it was that I didn't. While she's a perfectly cute lady, I don't know anyone who wants to look like Jennifer Aniston.

I had a horrible cold the night of our second date, but as NyQuil tends to make me agreeable, I just nodded along, zoning in and out of what he was saying. We'd gone to all these tony, upscale joints on our first date, so this time I'd forced him to meet me at one of my regular dives, fully aware that the jars of pickled eggs on the bar, blaring country music, and lack of drinks ending in "tini" would freak him right the fuck out. He walked into my local, took one horrified look at his surroundings, and hustled me right on outta there and into his waiting Beemer convertible.

At his car, I demonstrated my independent nature by opening my own door. That I could perform this feat of mechanical derring-do with no outside assistance never failed to astonish Larry. My "moxie" had been an issue on our first date as well. By our second, his shock and amazement that I was capable of performing tasks a chimp could handle with aplomb was starting to get on my nerves.

Seat belt fastened—did that myself too—we drove a block and a half to some funk-ay bar on Avenue C where they played music I hadn't realized anyone would listen to voluntarily.

After the southern Siberian throat singing laid over a techno beat started to give me an involuntary tic, I demanded we leave and dragged him to yet another smelly dump where I insisted on paying for drinks.

This had been a problem from jump. In sharp contrast to the usual mooks and losers I'd been dating, Larry took it as an insult to his masculinity every time my wallet emerged—it was like his dick shrunk another inch with every sawbuck I shelled out.

"I just can't get used to this women's lib stuff," he lamented as I shoved him out of the way to force my fiver on the bartender.

By now the NyQuil had worn off, and even a frosty cold domestic beverage wasn't doing the trick. I started to get pissed. I reminded him that he'd had approximately 45 years to get used to that "newfangled" women's lib and as he was only 41 he should be well adjusted to it by now.

Larry smiled indulgently and then asked me my thoughts on prenups. I told him that marrying someone with a built-in divorce clause seemed horribly cynical, and I'd rather not bother. "What if *you* were the one with more money?" he asked. Oh, like that would *never* happen. Asshole.

"With the guys I normally date, I usually *am* the one with more money!" I snarled, getting crankier by the second. I'd been feeling kind of saucy, albeit a tad congested, when I'd left the house that evening. Now I just felt poor and kind of shabby.

OK, it's embarrassing confession time: I had sex with Larry the antifeminist anyway. So shoot me; I wanted to see the inside of a rich guy's apartment. I also crept out of his Patrick Bateman–esque place at first light and immediately deleted his number from my phone. He called to "break up" with me via voice mail a couple days later.

Dacia, a 25-year-old grad student/sex worker activist, had a similarly distasteful experience dating the unenlightened (though unlike me, she managed to keep her pants on). "He showed up at the appointed meeting place and I felt instant not-attraction," she told me. "He was short. Mind you, I actually like men who are shorter than me and often wear heels around them, just because. However, he lied about his height, and I find lying about appearance kind of dumb—if we are going to meet up, I am going to find out, and I'm going to wonder about the sanity of the inse-cure person behind the lie."

However, we covered the height lie earlier; besides, that wasn't the part that really bugged Dacia. The two sat down for lunch, and because he made her laugh, Dacia began to forgive his stretching of the truth. Until he revealed "that the last book he read was about Hitler, who he thought was 'brilliant in his own way.'"

Hmm. Loverboy also shared that he considered Ronald Reagan a "tactical genius," leaving Dacia scrambling for a way out. "At this point, I am thinking that I need to end the date, and quickly." So she came up with a nice little lie, which quickly came unraveled, but by the time Rea-gan had come up, she was done caring if *he* thought *she* was a jerk.

Because I'm such a bad liar and will inevitably get caught in it, I generally advise against fibbing. But when you're trapped in Threat level Endive, extreme measures are sometimes called for.

YOUR EXIT STRATEGY

Some people might get all worked up and try to enlighten their politically abhorrent date, subscribing them to lefty mailing lists or attempting to humorlessly harangue their ideological foe into submission. The experienced dater knows when to cut their losses and have a little fun. I suggest you use your differences to your advantage when it comes to bidding your adieus:

- "Whoa, look at the time—I'm late for my abortion!"

- "Sorry, gotta run—Mom's getting out of prison this afternoon. She blew up an army recruitment office upstate, and the pigs got *soooo* uptight about it!"

- "Did you know that the average fart is made up of 59 percent nitrogen, 21 percent hydrogen, 9 percent carbon dioxide, 7 percent methane, and 4 percent oxygen? We are killing this planet through our asses!"

THE LEG HUMPER

You've been sitting with him for an hour and have yet to make eye contact because his eyes haven't left your tits. You're no prude, but you've removed his hand from your thigh/ass/neck four times before the appetizer even made its way to the table. Ladies and gentlemen, meet the Leg Humper.

Leg Humpers come in all shapes and sizes, and believe it or not, they're not always male. What they are is aggressive, inappropriate, and highly annoying.

Dawn, a 37-year-old registered nurse, met her first 'humper when she was home from college one summer. "I was waiting for my summer job as a camp counselor to start, and one lazy morning around 10, the doorbell rings, and I, in my bathrobe, look out the window to see the Greenscape truck on the street."

Being a city slicker, I was unsure what this meant, but Dawn explained: "Greenscape is one of those companies that pours chemicals over your lawn to make it grow a color green never found in nature, and for some reason my mom was letting them do this to our lawn every week." Oh.

"I answered the door and found an awkward, young, sort of cute guy around my age, standing there in his uniform."

Sounds like the beginning of a porno—who doesn't dig a man in uniform? "Half an hour or so later, there he is, the Greenscape Guy, back on my porch, this time to inform me he's done spraying. He lingered a moment, and while staring at his feet, asked me out on a date. I was too stunned (and too nice, I suppose) to say no, so I agreed."

Despite the fact that she said yes, Dawn didn't really want to go out with the guy. Her mom/pimp poured her a vodka tonic and pointed out that it was "just one date."

Beaten down and liquored up by her mom, Dawn went through with the date. "All through dinner Greenscape Guy is talking about all of the things we'll do together over the summer, making plans as though I'm his girlfriend."

Wait, didn't we meet this jumping-the-gun guy a few pages ago? Dawn continues, "I was getting irritated and explained to him—several times—I was going to be working at camp all summer and then returning to college in the fall, so there really wasn't a chance of us going out again. He was persistent, asking about days off, how long of a drive it was to my college . . . By the time dinner was over, I was sick of the Greenscape Guy and wishing the night was over."

But they still had a movie to see. The two of them got in the car "and all of a sudden he's climbing over the stick shift to kiss me, all wet and sloppy, and I'm pulling away, no longer irritated, but mad." As they walked into the theater the Landscaping Lothario pulled out a golden pickup line: "Let's sit in the back so we can make out."

Dawn demured, instead opting for a seat in the middle of the theater. "I spent the next two hours physically removing his hands from my body. I didn't even get to see most of the movie, as I was too occupied with defending myself from his groping advances."

After the film ended, Dawn kept her distance on the walk back to the car, counting the seconds till she could yell at her mom. "By this time I'm stiff with anger, and as I'm buckling my seat belt, the Greenscape Guy fires off great pickup line number 2: 'Is there anyplace good around here we can go to park?'"

Even a lunkhead like him can see he's getting nowhere, so on the drive home, he whips out the pity ploy (a sad, sad maneuver). "He tells me he just got out of the Marines and hasn't been with a woman in over two years. I was not moved to end his slump," Dawn reported with a chill in her voice.

Desperation set in. As they pulled up in front of Dawn's house, he tries what has to be the worst line in recorded history: "Can I at least touch your breast?" Dawn yelped a big fat negative. She was quick, but no match for a man possessed. "As I'm sliding out of the car, he reached over and grabbed it anyhow." Thanks, Mom!

As I mentioned earlier, Leg Humpers are not just of the male variety. Peter, a 56-year-old Massachusetts-based musician, found this out firsthand when he met a divorcée on JDate. "She was so helpful, it was really embarrassing," he told me in a phone interview. "She even knit me a scarf!"

Peter's complete disinterest in any kind of committed relationship is not something he shies away from talking about. He likes his alone time and can go weeks without seeing anyone he doesn't have to. But he is only human and sometimes gets lonely, so he IMs with various people he meets online.

Lady-date was one of those people. The two e-gabbed for a couple weeks and suddenly "she's decided she's going to move here," he said. "So all of a sudden, she has one interview after another, and somehow she has translated our IMing into a budding relationship, although I was very adamant about it not being that!"

The woman cajoled Peter into putting her up under the pretense of interviewing with prospective employers in his area. But once she got to his house it became obvious that free accommodations were the last thing on her mind. "I'd never met her before and suddenly she's naked!" he yelped, obviously still outraged. "Also, she'd gotten a complete bikini wax for the occasion, which I found very presumptuous." Peter was so put off he evicted his would-be girlfriend the next morning. And no, in case you're wondering, he didn't have sex with her.

Online dating can lead to all sorts of misunderstandings and presumptions as Norm, the journalist we met in Part Two, can attest. "The woman described herself as 'curvy,' and she and I hit it off online pretty well," he told me. But Norm had been dating long enough to know he had to meet someone in person before getting too into things. "So we met for dinner," he continued. "Now, at 6′ and 215 pounds, I'm a stocky white boy, and I like my women to be shaped like women. I had not thought that 'curvy' meant

6′2″, 315 pounds." (It's a well-documented fact that "curvy" and/or "Rubenesque" often translates to "just-plain-fat," but I guess Norm hadn't received that memo.)

Norm wasn't attracted to the woman, but neither was he a cad who'd bail on dinner because it wasn't with the girl of his dreams—especially since they'd had such a good online rapport. "Sure enough, the dinner chat was really fun. After the appetizer plates were cleared, she excused herself to go to the bathroom. When she came back, she came over to my side of the table and put her hands in my lap, then sat down.

"Weird, right?"

"Yeah, that's kind of odd," I answered.

"Then I saw what she had put there: her panties."

Oh, no. I felt myself turning purple with embarrassment on this poor, misguided woman's behalf.

How the hell do you get out of a situation like that, I wondered.

"I bundled them in my napkin, handed them to her with a 'you dropped something,' and while she blushed and ran to the bathroom, I paid $20 in cash to get the check immediately. We left and have never spoken since."

Um, I doubt that woman's left her apartment since.

It's always surprising when, like Norm, you're just out having a perfectly chaste evening, and things suddenly take a prurient turn. One woman who contacted me through my blog told me about being out with a seemingly sweet, soft-spoken guy who walked her home and gave her a kiss good night outside her door. All was warm and fuzzy until she told him she should be going inside, as it was getting late. "He says, 'How about saying hi.'" Jeta, the woman, wasn't sure what he meant.

"He looked down; I looked down," she wrote. "And there *it* was. *It* was just out there, taking a breather, saying 'hi.'"

But of all the Leg Humpers I've heard about, 35-year-old film exec Rose had the best/worst story. I'll just let her tell it:

I met him at the Hollywood Bowl, and he overheard me asking my friends if they'd brought any chocolate. So he volunteered to get me some and came back with twenty candy bars! So I figured I'd go out with him, even though I wasn't attracted to him. He seemed really nice.

My first indication that he was kind of strange was when he kept asking what kind of car I drive. I drive a 10-year-old Honda Civic and told him so. He kept saying he pictured me driving a BMW. Uh, no.

After dinner we go back to my place. And he's kissing me, and then, all of a sudden—WHOA!

I was wearing these super-low-cut jeans, and he'd reached around, stuck his finger down the back of my pants, and popped a finger up my butt!

Who goes there prior to elsewhere?! A conversation is required before you go there! Not to mention a relationship! It is definitely not first-date behavior—and then, to make things worse, he went from back to front!

I kicked him out and ran into the shower and thought, if I get a urinary tract infection, I'm going to hunt him down and kill him!

Hmm. I would say that an uninvited finger up the butt trumps the boob grab, the panty drop, the talking penis, *and* the unsolicited bikini wax. By far. Congratulations, Rose, you have dated the most repellent perv of the bunch!

YOUR EXIT STRATEGY

If your date's going to behave like a leg-humping dog, then he or she should be treated accordingly. According to Cesar Millan, the Dog Whisperer, humping is a way of showing dominance. You need to become the pack leader and shut the humper down! A firm thwack with a rolled-up news-paper and a loud "NO!" should do the trick. If that doesn't work, there's always pepper spray.

ARE WE HAVING WHINE WITH DINNER?

Mewling infants and blind kittens have every right in the world to be needy. After all, unless someone else feeds, clothes, and changes them, they will die. Your date, presumably, has mastered all these tasks on his or her own. Which is why it's just freaky when the guy you're having dinner with suddenly morphs into a diaper-clad toddler, clamoring for the kind of attention only a mother should ever be asked to provide.

John was someone my other friend John fixed me up with during a dark and lonely period in my dating history.

Friend John assured me that Date John would show me a good time and would definitely count himself lucky to be out with me. Who could resist an intro like that? Not I.

The first night we spoke on the phone, our conversation lasted two hours. He was funny and weird, but in what I thought was a good way. We had no idea what the other looked like, but Friend John had assured the both of us that neither of our faces would make babies cry. We made plans to meet the following week but kept the phone option open until then. I don't know about him, but I was really optimistic.

Until he called the next night. In sharp contrast to the charming lunatic I'd chatted with the evening prior, on this night Date John was very depressed. He'd had a bad day at work and wanted to talk about it at great length. I listened for a while but had plans with friends and nicely told him I had to get off the phone.

He flipped out. Date John could not believe I would "leave him" in such a state. He accused me of being selfish and cold and finally hung up on me. I was shocked but figured I'd dodged a bullet.

Dan Renzi's needy little surprise came a few weeks into one of his relationships. "We went out to dinner with some people he works with," he told me. "After a few drinks, he started complaining to everyone how I wasn't very domestic."

At first Dan thought his special friend was joking and played along: "I don't cook, don't clean, whatever, ha ha," Dan laughed.

Until his date announced to all gathered: "It's my dream to find someone who will fetch me my slippers and the morning paper. And *this* one"—and he pointed at Dan— "won't do it!" Not content to leave it at that, Dan's date then lamented, "I wish I could find someone who was domestic, but I never can."

Yoga teacher Betty had a similar experience with a guy she met at one of her many jobs. "Our first date went well until he asked me if I cooked, cleaned, and was nurturing," she laughed. "He said his ex-girlfriend would sense when he woke up in the middle of the night—he wakes up every two hours, every night—and would rub his back until he fell back asleep."

Betty shrugged it off until he called her two days after their date. Over e-mail, she described their conversation—

she is "AL" (Appalled Lady), and we will call him "WB" for
Widdle Baby:

> WB: *Why don't you come over here?*
>
> AL: *Uh, it's Sunday. I'm not a ho. (Subtext in my
> mind: you're not hot enough for me to be a ho!)
> Besides, I have to go to work early tomorrow.*
>
> WB: *When can I see you? (in a plaintive voice)*
>
> AL: *I don't know. I'm flying home to Kansas this
> Thursday for Christmas.*
>
> WB: *(Whining) Take a day off work for me!*
>
> AL: *EXCUSE ME?!?*
>
> WB: *Take a day off for me!*
>
> AL: *No.*
>
> WB: *Well what are you doing in the evenings?*
>
> AL: *I teach yoga.*
>
> WB: *EVERY NIGHT?*
>
> AL: *Well, on Tuesdays I have to do my own yoga.*
>
> WB: *Why do you have to do yoga if you're already
> teaching it?*
>
> AL: *Because when I teach, I'm not doing my own . . .*
>
> WB: *Well, if you want to see me you have to make
> time. If something's important to you, you make
> time for it.*

Don't Be This Dater: The Revenge Dater

Dating—OK, who am I trying to kid—sleeping with one person to get back at another is always a bad idea. I know running through his or her best friends after being cruelly cast aside can be tempting, but it rarely works out in your favor.

Kate found out the hard way when she was looking for a passive-aggressive way to break up with her girlfriend, Mandy.

"Mandy went away for the summer, and while we had a fairly open relationship, her one directive was that I *not* sleep with her friend Sandy." Can we guess what Kate did?

"From the moment we met, I knew Sandy was interested in me—it was so clear that whenever she was interested in someone, it was because she thought she could get something from them."

Kate found Sandy repellent, but, as she explains rather lamely, "She was so persistent! She persisted and persisted . . ." Heh. Anyway. During their summer apart Mandy managed to piss Kate off, and guess who welcomed her with open arms and thighs? "I succumbed to [Sandy's] social-climbing clutches," Kate laughed. Like every bad deed, this one did not go unpunished. "It was really weird—she wouldn't take her clothes off . . . obviously she had major issues."

After they were done, Sandy wanted to have a long talk about what had transpired. Unfortunately for her, it wasn't until then that Kate realized what a bad move sex with Sandy had been and practically ran out the door. In a moment of insta-karma, Kate jumped on her bike and was promptly chased down the street by a gang of kids trying to steal it. Oh, and Mandy came back in the fall, found out what had happened between Kate and Sandy, and promptly dumped Kate.

I've also pulled the revenge fuck, I mean *date*, though I didn't manage to get anyone mad at me but *me*.

I loved my mad Lithuanian sculptor man. He was a brooding artist type whom every single one of my friends hated on sight. Predictably, I completely lost my shit over him. Huge blue eyes, big Mick Jagger mouth—just being within the same four-block radius as him made my brain sweat. Of course he didn't love me back, and the night after our best date ever, he finally broke it off with these words:

"This can't happen again. I have no good in my heart."
Huh? What was that supposed to mean—you have no good
in your heart? Being a mysterious, foreign artist type he
just shrugged and looked off all tortured-like.

I was devastated—so devastated that I fucked his best
friend, who had the added bonus of being his roommate.
Calvin had often offered me comfort and advice many times
during my torturous tenure with his friend. One night he
offered me something more. We went back to my place,
where I was confronted with the hugest penis I have ever
seen on any living animal.

I know girls are supposed to love big dicks, but
this was actually too big. It was like a flesh-colored fire
hydrant attached to his pelvis. And that wasn't the only
ugly surprise. As his pants fell to the floor, I noted he
was sporting a fashionable set of tan, thigh-high support
hose—you know, the kind your granny wears. And no, he
didn't remove them during sex either.

Even worse than that, the condom broke, giving me
both an AIDS *and* a pregnancy scare, and my intended
target of revenge never even found out. Or if he did, he
didn't care enough to mention it.

AL: *It's a little early in our relationship for you to be emotionally manipulative—*
WB: *I'm not! I'm just saying, if it's important, you make time for it!*

Betty wisely hung up on him. "This man did not want a girlfriend," she informed me. "He wanted a wet nurse. I could already feel him energetically rooting at my tit like a litter of piglets."

My story doesn't end nearly as cleverly as Betty's. Date John called the next day and apologized profusely (though he later confessed that he was still angry I'd chosen my friends over his boring work drama). Against my better judgment, I agreed to go out with him and indeed, suffered through a brief relationship with him. You'll meet him later in this section and again in Part Four, with the rest of the scary freaks.

YOUR EXIT STRATEGY

If your mom is sick and needs you to drop everything and run to the store for Theraflu, you do it. If some mook you just met wants you to rearrange your life according to his whims, you make like Nancy Reagan and just say no. Because no matter how much you do for these types, I promise you, it'll never be enough. Oh, and being polite as you exit just gives them an excuse to argue and whine some more. Shut it down.

THE SELF-PROMOTER

I am not famous. I have no delusions of grandeur and, truth be told, no desire to *get* famous. I write a column that has run in several small newspapers, but the overwhelming majority of people on this planet have no idea who I am, and I am fine with this. Unfortunately, even a teensy little outlet like a free weekly attracts people who want to manipulate you into helping them.

Jeff was a terminally depressed filmmaker who'd contacted me through Friendster or MySpace or Nerve or some other portal. You know those types who are always in crisis—they're either getting evicted or they have a weird lump on their foot or their electricity got cut off because the power company "hates" them? That was Jeff. We went out a couple times, and the romantic potential between us was so null and void I never even considered it. He just seemed to want a friend, which was fine with me.

But our conversations were never very interesting, which made me wonder why I bothered. Jeff talked a lot, but he didn't listen or ask any questions that didn't relate directly back to him—for example, "What do you think of my new short film?" One day he called, furious over something I'd tossed off in a column—not at all about him—and all his resentments about how little I'd done for him and his fantastic film career came pouring out in one abusive rant. I guess he'd been holding in his hatred for me until he figured out that I wasn't going to be able to turn him into the next Martin Scorsese. Duh.

Felicia Sullivan, a memoirist who edits a literary journal called *Small Spiral Notebook*, had a similar experience with a similarly ill-informed suitor. "I had just gotten out of a relationship with this horrible human being who unfortunately still exists," she told me in a phone conversation. "I thought after three months I was ready to date." She probably was. Like so many of us, she put a profile up on a dating site.

"This guy wrote me—he was gorgeous, articulate, well read, and we had this amazing e-mail banter. I was all excited and we decided to meet for drinks. And indeed, he was as gorgeous as he looks in his picture. He worked in advertising but told me, 'I have a corporate job, but I'm literate. . .'"

So what he's saying is that he has money, but he's also creative? I asked.

"Exactly," she answered.

"So we sit down, and literally, for about an hour, the only topic of conversation is *him*. If there's a point where he takes a breath and I interject, he cuts me off and says something like, 'That reminds me of a time I was surfing in Guatemala.' He just completely ignores and cuts me off."

Despite his good looks, Felicia was, understandably, not having a great time. "All he's talking about is himself and how all these women are falling all over him, but he's looking for the right girl."

Then he mentioned that he'd seen Felicia's literary journal. "I thought this was a turning point, and he was maybe going to ask me some questions!" she laughed.

Fat chance. Instead, "He whips out a CD and goes, 'I'm also in a band!'"

Of course he is. Not only that, she continued, "There's a girl in a leopard thong on the cover and across the thing in red writing is 'Smack. Dat. Ass.'"

"He hands it to me and goes, 'Think Kid Rock.'"

Mr. Smack Dat Ass promptly asked her to review it in her magazine. Hello? Do we need to define "literary" for you?

Felicia got feisty and snarled, "What do you know about *me*? Because the last forty-five minutes were all about *you*!"

Their date quickly degenerated into a loud argument, and yet as Felicia got up to leave he implored, "Aren't you going to review my CD?!?" She turned on her heel and walked out.

Predictably, that wasn't the end of the Ass Smacker. "For about two weeks he left about twenty voice mails and twelve e-mails, not about how we should date again, but about how I left my copy of *Smack Dat Ass* behind at the restaurant!"

YOUR EXIT STRATEGY

Parasites who are only looking out for themselves are one of the easiest types to rid yourself of. Just tell them you're quitting your job (or whatever it is about you that makes them think you're a mark) and plan on dedicating yourself to helping the homeless. Promptly hit them up for a donation and watch as they skedaddle.

THE CRITIC

Kate Moss is my ideal woman—you'll really be needing to lose some weight if you expect this to work," suggested Date John, the short, graying, pudgy, presumptuous man I first described in the section on closet cases. While it's true that I—like most women—am *way* fatter than Kate Moss and could stand to lose some weight, it wasn't like I'd gained any since I met him. John was just one of those jerky types who always had advice on how you could make yourself "better." Not that anybody had asked him.

I'm sure you're familiar with the type.

Nicole, a 19-year-old student from San Francisco, had the misfortune of meeting one of these helpful souls online. "He picked me up on a Friday night, and he seemed kinda cold—much harsher than he had seemed on IM and the phone. After saying hello, we barely spoke the whole way there."

"There" was a café where the two of them spent what sounds like a wrenching thirty minutes listening to a band neither of them could stand. Nicole's date made it clear he didn't like her. "I would try to bring up topics and short funny comments, and he would kill them, every time." After sitting in an uncomfortable silence for a while longer, they decided to cut the evening short. "We got on the freeway, and he sped ahead of a few cars getting ready to merge on. I was a little surprised by such acceleration and asked him about his car."

Her date's reply: "Yeah. You would be surprised how fast this thing can go. There's just too much weight in it right now; it's normally just my friend and I in here."

Gulp. Not surprisingly, Nicole was mortified. "I'm not huge, but at that moment, I felt like I should have had Jenny Craig on my speed dial."

Culinary student Anni lasted ten months with someone who complained she was too fat. "He was constantly telling me to lose weight and held out in the sack for *ten* months!" When she finally dumped his nasty, withholding ass (thank you!) he told her, "Would you want to sleep with someone that hurts you when they are on top of you?" Nice. I guess her current boyfriend isn't such a delicate flower because he seems pretty happy.

When I fixed Marissa up with a handsome friend of mine named Clay, I knew there was no guarantee they'd hit it off. But while Clay was grateful for my effort, Marissa was furious that I'd matched her with someone who had, as she called them, "girly hands." Having been distracted by his otherwise good looks and sparkling wit, I'd never noticed his hands. I still don't know what she's talking about because she quit talking to me.

Here's a tip—if you don't like the way someone looks, don't go out with them.

YOUR EXIT STRATEGY

You could take the low road and go right for your critic's Achilles heel, because believe me, people overly concerned with your shortcomings are never without several dozen of their own. They just compensate by looking outward. But insulting someone back is a waste of your time and energy. A simple "piss off" should suffice.

THE CRAZY, LEVEL II

Crazy is one of those conditions that can escalate from kind of quirky and entertaining to downright scary very quickly. My buddy Bob found this out the hard way one Easter morning a few years ago. "I'd been dating this woman who was a great deal older than me," he told me. "I knew she was kind of weird, but I liked her at first."

The Saturday night leading into Easter found the two of them drinking heavily in front of her TV screen. "She kept wanting me to eat this Easter egg she'd made, but hard-boiled eggs and beer . . . I wasn't interested." His date insisted, but asked him to eat it over the sink so he wouldn't make a mess. Bob was confused, but did as he was told. (One of the myriad good things about dating younger men—they're obedient.)

Bob cracked the shell on the side of the sink and watched in horror as the egg emptied blood all over his hands! All the while, his date cackled maniacally. He left immediately and never spoke with her again. Never did find out how she pulled that trick either.

Of course, once again, Rich can be counted on to bring the crazy. I feel I should mention that Rich and I met through Nerve.com. We went on one friendly but chemically inert date and decided we were better off as friends. After hearing his tales of woe, I'm convinced it could've never worked out between us because I am not nearly batshit loony enough for him.

Rich met this particular wacko after she scoped him out on the subway, back before he deserted New York City for the semi–Deep South. We'll call this chick Pecan, for reasons that will soon become obvious. Over their romantic dinner together, "she admitted to chronic fatigue syndrome, arthritis, a nervous breakdown, that she's seeing a therapist, and taking unspecified medications. I repeat, all over dinner."

After two glasses of wine with dinner, two beers with vodka chasers after, and an apple martini nightcap, Rich suspected she might also have a drinking problem in addition to her other "issues." "Then we had to walk to the store for more beer to bring home. She also asked me to buy her a bottle of vodka, which I didn't." Thus clearing up any ambiguity about her alcoholic status.

Once they got back to her apartment—you didn't think he was going to just turn and go home after all that?—Pecan informed him that she was part of a coven and was fond of performing different rituals that Rich was too spooked to

How Not to Date a Shrink

Rob Dobrenski, PhD: Therapist and founder/writer, Shrinktalk.net

Okay, so you're out having drinks with friends and it turns out the guy you've got your eye on is a therapist. What's the exact wrong thing to say to him/her?

Oh, where to start . . . "Are you going to analyze me? Ha ha!" "I should have been a shrink, but I'm just too crazy, ha ha!" "Oh, could I tell you some stories about my family, ha ha!" and "Aren't all shrinks messed up themselves? Ha ha!" All these have all been said time and time again. Unfortunately, they weren't funny the first time.

My shrink is really hot—should I go for it?

Unless you thoroughly enjoy rejection, under no circumstances should you go for it—99.9 percent of shrinks will decline such advances. In fact, if you have a good working relationship with your shrink, that is likely to be damaged as well, because it's very hard to go back to keeping it professional once you've made an attempt at seduction. If you do decide to take your chances, be prepared for many sessions to discuss your "conscious and subconscious motivations" for doing so. And if you happen to find that 0.1 percent without ethics, ask yourself: what else isn't he ethical about?

Okay, blah, blah, I knew you'd say that was a bad idea and that no ethical therapist would go there—but how do I get him to bend those pesky rules? (Not that you'd ever do that, but theoretically speaking.)

In the therapist's world, one is guilty until proven innocent. That means that if the state's licensing board discovered a dual relationship, it would assume that psychological damage to the patient has occurred and will reprimand the professional accordingly. This usually means taking away that therapist's license, sometimes permanently. Therefore, if you want to get your therapist to date you, convince him that you mean more to him than the five-plus years of graduate school he trudged through, as well as his livelihood.

Do you think most therapists prefer their dates in therapy or already sane?
This is a trick question, as it implies that someone in therapy is not sane. Some of the most psychologically healthy people I know are currently in therapy, and good therapists know that psychotherapy can be a great outlet for personal growth. I would imagine that most therapists are attracted to people who have at least been in therapy at some point in their lives, as they usually have some great insights into themselves. Plus, it's great to come home to someone who knows what your day might have been like!

What about meds? How long do you wait before revealing your SSRI Rx?
Even in 2007, there still exists a stigma around seeking help for psychiatric problems. Many still erroneously see medication as only for the "crazy" or "weak." Also, many medications are written "off-label," meaning that they are prescribed for something other than their originally intended use. I don't write scripts myself, but I have many patients, for example, who take antipsychotics for sleep or extreme agitation, even if they aren't psychotic. However, many men will balk at hearing

"Wow, my Haldol is mixing with this wine nicely!" on a first encounter. In other words, you might want to find out what your date knows about psychiatric medicine before throwing back a Valium in front of him.

I imagine when new people—even attractive people you're thinking of dating—find out what you do, they sometimes make inappropriate disclosures. What's the worst you've heard?
The topper happened when I was in graduate school, when I was introduced to a woman at a party. Upon hearing what I was studying, she assumed that I could send subliminal messages from my brain to her genitals, which would force her to have sex with me. She stumbled away, drunk and angry, referring to me as a "Rapist Incognito."

Is it wrong to ask your shrink/date for a freebie session?
An ethical therapist will always say no, but if you bat your eyelashes and imply that you'll make it worth his while, it's a great way to flirt!

What's more impressive and why—a potential date with years of Freudian analysis under her belt or someone who's never considered therapy and thinks it's for "crazies"?
Without a doubt, the woman in therapy (in clinical circles, "the analysand") is more desirable. Although some people who have done years of true analysis, which is traditionally at least three times per week, can be very self-absorbed (do you need to talk about yourself that much?), anyone with knowledge about the process and outcome of therapy will score major points over the ignoramus.

inquire about further. But my favorite little Pecan nugget is this: "She has five cats and makes up pretend baby voices for each of them. She'd ask the cat a question and then say the answer in her pretend baby voice, insisting that this was actually the cat talking. This didn't happen once, but several times," he told me.

YOUR EXIT STRATEGY

Crazy people are easy to get rid of. Especially when they fully believe their pets have the power of speech. Simply pick up your phone, punch in some numbers, and have a conversation with your "dog" at the other end. Announce that Mr. Scrambles is really depressed, and you need to pick up his meds and a doughnut, so you'll have to be going.

THE CHEAPSKATE, LEVEL III

We're going to segue right into more fun with Rich! I think you'll agree my friend has a rare gift for attracting the freaks. Blessedly, this date only lasted for a few short hours.

"I took this woman to the wax museum," he told me over whiskeys during a visit. "She insisted on paying for herself." So far, so good; Rich wanted to pay, but she kept insisting, so he told her that if spending money was that important, she could get dinner.

What Rich didn't realize was that her offer to pay had been a test. She informed him over pasta (which he also paid for) that "no manly man would even consider the woman paying an option" and that if they started "courting," he would be expected to pay for *everything*—from her phone bill to dinners out to clothes for her. Bear in mind that while Rich isn't poor, he is the custodial parent of two teenage girls—he's got *their* phone and T.J. Maxx bills to worry about.

Ms. Snippy went on to inform him that "the last man she went out with—whom, oddly enough, she considered too controlling—would never let her pay. They wouldn't do *anything* if *he* couldn't afford to pay for it."

Foolish Rich hadn't realized that there was a time travel machine at the wax museum that shot them back to 1952. First date, last date.

Michelle was so entrenched with her skinflint, she went so far as to get engaged—sans ring, naturally—to the guy. "We'd been dating for about a month when I had my thirtieth birthday," she confided. "He bought me a box of bow tie pasta, because I once said it was my favorite kind. Cost: $1.20." But her stingy suitor wasn't done. He also bought his lucky lady a tube of KY Jelly. "Apparently he thought the pasta would excite me enough to want to do him on the front seat of his truck!" she laughed.

YOUR EXIT STRATEGY

There is one quick way to get rid of a cheapskate—turn the tables and show up to meet with only enough money in your wallet to pay for yourself. Or none at all. My nonscientific studies have shown that people who are stingy one way are generally less than generous in other arenas as well.

PART FOUR

ABANDON HOPE ALL YE WHO ENTER HERE

THREAT LEVEL: CAROB

You're going to rub elbows with the elite—pimps, addicts, thieves, bums, winos, girls who can't keep an address, and men who don't care.

—Sergeant Joe Friday, *Dragnet*

PART FOUR:
ABANDON HOPE ALL YE
WHO ENTER HERE

THREAT LEVEL: CAROB

If there were a *Dater Dragnet*, just about everyone you're going to read about in this section would be rotting behind bars for crimes against romance. While there's no doubt dating is not for the faint of heart, the men and women creepy enough to make it into threat level Carob have shocked and awed—and not in a good way—even this well-seasoned dating professional.

The most insidious thing about these types is that they possess the ability to come off as normal, attractive daters, which is how they lure unsuspecting victims like you or I into going out with them in the first place. But scratch lightly at their shallow veneer, and you'll find a ticking time bomb of misery.

Normally I suggest sticking out even the most boring date for at least forty-five minutes before making a gracious exit. While this is a nice idea in theory, there are some instances where you just have to cut and run. These are some of them. If you find yourself in any of the situations described in the next few pages, you have my permission to get up and leave. I don't care if you're in the middle of dinner or the movie's just started—get out. Leave. Vamoose. There are some things worse than being rude. These are but a few . . .

GROSS!

Have you ever been out with someone whose behavior— whether on purpose or inadvertently—makes you feel like you've got a wad of wet cat hair wrapped around your uvula? No? Count yourself lucky.

Joanne thought she'd won the Boyfriend Lotto when she met Jim. He was handsome and employed—what more could a girl want? Until they went out for coffee, and he spent the whole time picking at the seat of his pants. We're not talking about a little pull-the-wedgie-out either. We're talking digging—as if there was gold in that there ravine.

My friend Mark also dated a man with wandering hands, only instead of his butt, Mark's date came back from a restroom visit with his hands down the front of his trousers. At first Mark thought his friend was just making an adjustment. I hear that when you're a guy sometimes things shift where they're not supposed to, and a little rejiggering is called for. Except that his rearranging lasted the rest of the night. They'd be talking and Mr. Weiner just kept rubbing up on the rod and tackle. Mark is admittedly a bit of a slut and probably would've excused this behavior if it'd been just the two of them. But self-frottage in front of the waitress? Yuck. Mark started to wonder if his date was hosting insect life down below, which promptly killed any thoughts of romance.

Of course nastiness can also be found above the belt. "I was once on the fence about a guy I was seeing," started Mary, a 23-year-old I found doing online research. "He met his brutal end because of a booger hanging from his nose." A bat in the cave could happen to anyone, but this dude's nasal emission came with unfortunate timing. "We were having sex, and it dangled on the edge of his nostril, all wet and green!" she e-shrieked. "Somehow telling him seemed more embarrassing to me, so I just kicked him out after he came and never spoke to him again." Nice of her to wait until he got off.

Mary also dated a guy who, as she describes it, "ate like he had not eaten in a month. He literally shoveled food into his mouth, lifting the plate to be closer for his face for shoveling!" Though not as repulsive as the boogeyman, Mary also gave him the heave-ho for eating like an extra on *Oz*.

"Basic manners are a must! I could not bring this guy to a company dinner or to meet my family—the end."

Anni went out with a guy who farted in front of her on the first date, but Marjorie had hands down the worst of the worst: "The date was so awkward we spent the whole time getting severely wasted," she explained. "So much so that even though I wasn't attracted to him, I let him come back to my apartment." Bad idea, Marjorie.

"We kept drinking," she continued. "We were out on the fire escape and he kissed me." Uh-oh . . . wait for it . . .

"As soon as his mouth came away from mine, he started vomiting violently over the railing." All together now—ewwwww!!!!!

How Not to Date a Torch Singer

Peg Simone: *The Deeper You Get*

Do you get many male groupies?
I think men are afraid of me. They tend to stare in a way that makes me not quite sure as to whether they're interested or appalled.

What is the WORST line anyone's ever used on you?
It's not quite a line, but a man once tried to turn me on by raising his hands in claw-like gestures and then began to growl.

What is the one thing a guy who's trying to hit on you should NOT say?
"I can't find the woman I love, so I've been with many women." This was actually said to me, to which I replied, "Good for you, I guess."

He replied, "Yes, yes, very good for me." Not only impressed with his own bravado but also entirely clueless!

If you met someone you were interested in, would you prefer he already be a fan of your music or have not ever heard it or seen you play?
I think it would be nice to meet someone who is totally unrelated to what I do; however, a fan could always be good for the ego. Especially if that fan were Bruce Springsteen or Gael Garcia Bernal.

Are there any Peg Simone fashion dealbreakers?
Lots of (I hate to even say this word) "bling." Oh, and those pants that fall below a guy's ass—they just make me want to run over and pull them up. I would also have to add facial piercings to that list; they look uncomfortable and seem rather high maintenance.

DON'T BE THAT DATER

Speaking as someone who once fell out of a chair, farted as her ass hit the ground, and then topped off the charm sundae by running to the bathroom and vomiting at the end of one particularly enchanted evening, I can tell you with confidence, most foulness can be avoided if you keep the alcohol intake, if not to a minimum, at least to a level where you don't lose control. Keeping tissues, a hand mirror, and breath mints on your person at all times is also not such a bad idea. If you're prone to being a Gassy Gus, add a discreet bottle of Beano to the mix.

BAD BOYS (AND GIRLS)

Right up there with "enjoys long walks on the beach," the most irritating cliché one can stick in their online dating profile is that they're seeking a "partner in crime." Only someone with zero experience dating actual criminals would write such a thing. Of course, these wayward daters don't actually mean they're seeking someone to accompany them on a felony or three, but when you've actually witnessed a boyfriend get hauled off to the pokey, the humor gets lost.

We all make mistakes. And true, sometimes those errors in judgment come at a price (incarceration). While there's certainly nothing wrong with those who have paid their debt to society, criminals—convicted or otherwise—aren't always who we should be dating.

Valerie, a 51-year-old HR manager from Toronto, found herself on the wrong side of the law with an old high school crush. "He was totally hot in high school, but I was nerdy and we never ran with the same crowd, so I was ecstatic when, years later, he asked me out for dinner," she explained over e-mail.

Val got all gussied up and met him at his apartment for drinks. "It was a grotty little bachelor walk-up, but his walls were covered with amazing artwork—the real deal— Picasso, Jackson Pollock, etcetera. He said he was an art dealer," Valerie continued.

The combination of expensive art and nasty apartment should've set off warning bells, but Val was that most deadly combination of naive and infatuated.

"I sit down, expecting a nice glass of wine, but instead he whips out a mirror and proceeds to cut some huge lines.

I didn't and don't do coke, so I politely declined while he blew his nostrils out."

Meanwhile, the guy's phone was ringing off the hook. Her date explained it must be an annoying client and suggested they go for a walk. "I guess all the coke had made him forget about the dinner we were supposed to have."

The two walked aimlessly for an hour and wound up at a trendy rooftop bar of an elegant hotel. "Now this was more like it! We had a few drinks, some chat, some kisses . . ."

Then things took an unwelcome turn. "The hotel was undergoing renovations, and there were some beautiful antique mirrors leaning against the wall, waiting to be installed," Val wrote. "Suddenly, he got a weird gleam in his eye and said, 'Hey, nobody's around, help me get these down to the street!'"

Her date then proceeded to stiff the bar for their drinks and drag a stolen mirror over to the elevator, fully expecting she'd grab the other end and join him on his crime spree.

"I stood there stunned and blurted something about taking a different elevator, as I didn't want to be caught stealing," she continued. Val got to the lobby and took off running.

"I didn't return any of his phone calls after that."

But not every inexcusable crime is a felony. The occasional misdemeanor can also be a deal breaker. New Yorker Jen Dziura dated one such minor-league bad guy and didn't risk arrest in the process.

"The Russian was a large, pale, beefy fellow with a girlish laugh and a dubious sense of morality," she told me. "When I finally took him back to my place—an ill-advised maneuver to begin with—he told me how much he hated condoms."

Make no mistake: this guy wasn't that stupid—he was willing to wear them but "refused to pay for condoms, as he didn't want to contribute to this sexual travesty with his dollars." So instead Jen's date—who, P.S., was a highly paid banker—*stole* condoms from the local drug store. "He thought of this as an act of civil disobedience," she laughed. "I pointed out that young men with Ivy League degrees who work for major investment banks are basically incapable of performing genuine acts of civil disobedience. Then we had sex."

Of course, as these stories are wont to go, this wasn't all. "Afterward, he opened my fifth-floor bedroom window, removed the [stolen] condom, and gleefully tossed it out the window."

Yuck. "Oh my God!" Jen exclaimed. "That's going to be there forever!" She peered out the window and saw it leaking onto the roof of the single-story Latin music store next door.

"I know!" her Russian tittered with glee.

While yes, a coke-snorting thief and a rubber robber are probably not people you'll want to be seeing again, as Norm, the journalist who was given the gift of the big-girl underpants in Part Three, discovered, things could be worse.

"I was dating online, and a woman who had no ad of her own answered mine," Norm reported, appropriately, via e-mail. "After a bit of back and forth, I suggested that we meet for a proper date." Their first date went fine. "She was cute but quite reserved. About two days after our first date, she e-mailed and suggested another."

This time, instead of coffee, they agreed to go to a local pool hall. "We got a table, and I offered to get her a beer." Her reply: 'I don't drink. And I don't approve of people who do.'" Ooh, snap!

Don't Be This Dater: The "Nice" Guy

You're probably thinking to yourself, "Judy, why are you advising people to stay away from nice guys? Aren't nice guys, by definition, kind and gentle? Are you saying that women really should only go out with bad guys?"

No. That's not what I'm saying. Note the quotation marks surrounding the word "nice." As a dating columnist, I hear from rageaholics constantly, and the worst offenders are those who bill themselves as "nice" yet are consumed with so much rage it practically jumps off the computer screen and pops me one in the face. These guys act as though refraining from being a serial killer should be enough to have the ladies dropping at their feet.

Take, for instance, this psycho who wrote in to my column, furious when a fix-up didn't result in a love connection: "I guess I'm supposed to die of a hard-on for the privilege of buying Miss Glamour-Puss lunch. So much for Mr. Nice Guy; maybe I should have drug her off, broke her like a shotgun, and horse-fucked her? Maybe that's what she really wanted."

This guy is clearly deranged—coffee gone wrong ends up in thoughts of rape and battery? One of the many things that makes his letter so chilling is that this isn't some bunker-dwelling lunatic—this guy actually has friends! Friends who are willing to fix him up with *their* friends! Not only that, this dude obviously considers himself a catch. And lest you think this is one isolated creep, I get letters in a similar vein several times a year, all penned by men who consider themselves the epitome of "nice." You have to wonder which dictionary they're consulting.

So, to clear up any confusion, I've devised a chart to help you discern an actual nice guy from his faker cousin, the "nice" guy.

"NICE" GUY

- Drones on about what a great, giving, enlightened guy he is and how he never catches a break because women just want to go out with jerks. The undercurrent of bitterness is so palpable it may cause your mouth to pucker.

- His biggest assets are negatives that he shares with you constantly: He *doesn't* cheat, *doesn't* believe in hitting girls (thanks!), he's *not* an alcoholic or a drug addict, etcetera.

- Fully believes that the above "qualities" have earned him nothing short of supermodels with Mensa-level IQs. Any woman who falls short of his exacting standards is invisible to him. He wouldn't dream of having a female friend. (Though to be fair, nor would any thinking lady bother befriending him.)

- When you ask him what he feels like doing, he'll shrug and tell you he's up for anything. But once you come up with a plan, he spends the next three weeks complaining about it.

- Spends a lot of time examining his "dark side," mistaking self-obsession for self-awareness.

THE ACTUAL NICE GUY

- Doesn't *talk* about being kind; he just *is*. He realizes that not being a jerk isn't enough to warrant him his own personal awards ceremony.

- His biggest assets are positives: He listens when you talk, has an interesting life, is genuinely interested in other people, and is unfailingly polite.

- He likes a wide variety of women and doesn't have an ironclad "type." He has female friends.

- If you ask him what he feels like doing, he has actual ideas. If he's up for following your lead he does so, if not cheerfully, at least with a sense of humor.

- Doesn't take himself too seriously. Especially when he knows he's wrong.

- Speaking of wrong, the actual nice guy acknowledges the occasional mistake.

- Realizes that everybody gets dumped and it's rarely for being too nice.

Norm informed her that teetotaling was not in his future and offered to take her home. She told him, "I've decided I really don't like you, but I don't want to stop dating you."

Red flag! Run, Norm, run!

Norm stayed. "We played pool for a while, and after her third or so snide comment about beer drinking, I decided that I would drink a bit more aggressively (or is it passive-aggressively?)."

Norm upped his beer intake until she finally said it was time for her to go home. Being a (slightly drunk) gentleman, Norm offered to walk her home. "She lived in a creepy neighborhood about fifteen blocks from where we were." He told her if she wasn't comfortable with that, he'd pay for a cab.

"She refused both and told me she'd be fine walking. I told her that I wasn't *walking her home*" [wink, wink!], "but actually walking her home. I even offered to walk ahead or behind or across the street from her."

After a hostile back and forth, she finally relented but refused to tell Norm her address. "We walked in silence to her hood. As we turned onto one dimly lit street, she ran two houses down, sprinted up the stoop, waved 'Bye now!' and dashed inside. I noticed a sign on the lawn. I went over to read it." Uh-oh.

Ever the reporter, Norm googled the name of the place the second he got home. "It was a halfway house," he informed me. Through his foggy beer goggles, Norm started to notice the crimson flags that had been waving in his face for the last couple hours.

"As a former paralegal, I knew my way around Lexis-Nexis. I searched her name and found out she had been released from prison six months earlier after a six-year stint for . . . killing her husband."

Not surprisingly, Norm never saw his date again. Guess she simply couldn't abide dating a drinker.

Clarissa met her criminal at the record store they both worked at. "He was a security guard—pretty cute and only a few years older than me," she reported. "He had an incredibly intense energy and always had an opinion about everything. But he was sweet and clearly liked me."

Bravely ignoring the common knowledge about crapping where you eat, Clarissa agreed to go out with him.

At a local bar they chatted. Things were going well until "after a little small talk and gossip about work, he told me about the two people he had killed."

Um, what?

"The first was someone who was trying to mug him. This guy was a huge karate nerd, very into physical fitness and kickboxing. So when someone tried to mug him at knifepoint, he struggled with the mugger and ended up stabbing him in the neck."

Figuring you might be able to chalk that one up to self-defense, Clarissa cautiously inquired about the second body. "That was when he was working as a guard at our store— maybe a year before I started," she continued. "There was a drunk homeless guy who would come in and shoplift, but they had never been able to catch him. Until one time, my date actually sees him pocket a DVD and chases him out of the store. The guy apparently hid behind a Dumpster with a brick, laying in wait for my friend, and bashed him in the face. My friend proceeded to kick the shit out of the guy. Perhaps weakened by his various drug- and booze-related health problems, the shoplifter actually died."

Holy cow. "First date! Killed two people!"

Not surprisingly their date ended shortly after that revelation. "He walked me back home like a total gentleman, and we proceeded to have several awkward months working together until I left that job." It's not like she could say anything. Who wants to piss off a murderer?

DON'T BE THAT DATER

I realize that everyone makes mistakes. However, if you're going to lead a life of crime, don't drag your unsuspecting date down to central booking with you. If you have a criminal past, reveal it like you would an STD: after you've decided to sleep with them, but *before* any clothing comes off.

DOA (DRUNK ON ARRIVAL)

Few things are less appealing than a suitor who shows up for your big date slurring and wobbling. Being with someone who's drunk when you're sober is like trying to decipher Mandarin spoken with a Croatian accent.

Paul from Nebraska had the misfortune of dating a lightweight with a personality disorder. "She was totally blasted after two drinks, underwent some sort of transformation right there, and started calling me an asshole."

Neato! At least David, a 40-year-old fiction writer from Brooklyn, had a more interesting experience:

Before I became friends with my friend Nicole, we went out on a date. We go out, and I know Nicole is a little wild, which is why I wanted to go out with her. At the time she was doing a lot of Ecstasy. I don't know what she was high on, all I know is we went to some Indian restaurant . . .

I knew we were going to get wild because she was doing shots of Jack Daniels with Jack-and-Coke chasers. Then she went to the bathroom—she might've been high on Ecstasy—and came back acting all crazy. We're in this little tiny restaurant, and she's a big girl, and the next thing I know she's got her leg up on the wall.

I just decided to grin and bear it. Then she asks, "Are you embarrassed by me?" I said no, but she could tell it was a lie, so she goes into this tirade!

"Fuck these people! I don't care what they think!" she's yelling. All the waiters and other patrons are staring. We leave, and of course, I can't just go my separate way—I have to see if I can hit it.

We're in a cab, and we start kissing, and she bites my tongue really hard! I jumped back and asked her why she did that, and she just started laughing this wicked laugh. I'm not a smart guy, so I try to kiss her again. She bit my tongue again.

Then we go to this bar filled with all these model chicks and the people who love them. Her friend Miesha comes over to me and goes, "Well, how was your date?"

I said it was terrible. She asked why. I said it was a ménage à trois. She looked puzzled. I tell her: me, Nicole, and Jack Daniels.

Film exec Rose had a date come to pick her up only to discover he was stoned out of his mind on pot brownies a neighbor had fed him. "I felt too guilty to make him go home, so I suggested a brisk walk around the neighborhood, thinking the fresh air might clear his head." No such luck. Harry the Hemp Eater informed her that "if we're gonna have sex, we have to be careful because I have herpes." Charming! Rose laughed, "Those must've been some good brownies, because he thought he was going to get laid!"

DON'T BE THAT DATER

Melvin was someone who contacted me on Nerve.com. With his penchant for gold chains and shiny shirts, he was pretty much the exact opposite of anyone I'd normally go out with. I declined his offer politely, but still he persisted, wondering why a smart, pretty woman like me wouldn't go out with him. My first mistake was writing him back, because, using a combination of flattery and self-deprecation, he talked me into giving him my phone number. My second mistake was answering the phone. Note: It's much easier to turn someone down over e-mail.

During our brief phone chat he continued with the flirting and then basically accused me of having something against Jewish intellectuals.

Oy vey! He'd found my weak spot. You know how some girls get all quivery in the kneecaps over basketball players or stockbrokers? I've always had a thing for neurotic Jewish smarty-pants—think a young Woody Allen without the whole daughter-schtupping nonsense. Mrow.

I decided to overlook the gold chain and meet him for a drink. What could it hurt?

In the days prior to our date, Melvin kept up a steady stream of unreciprocated e-flirtation. The more he "talked," the more I began to dread being stuck in the same room as him. Just as people who describe themselves as hilarious will rarely make you crack a smile, Melvin helped me discover that men who tout themselves as "intellectuals" are generally kind of, well, stupid.

Instead of doing the brave thing and feigning an illness, or blowing him off and never answering my phone again, I decided to join my friend Heather for a preload prior to meeting him. As she was a bartender at the time, this quickly got *ugly*.

By the time I showed up—an hour late, at another bar, naturally—to meet Melvin, I was slightly left of tipsy but not quite full-on wasted. Even in my nearly inebriated state, Melvin was not hard to spot. In fact, his full-body dousing of Axe cologne, snug slacks, and shiny gold *chai* pendant made him impossible to miss.

I wobbled over to his table, plunked my ass down, ordered a drink, and promptly removed his hand from my knee.

"What do you think you're doing?" I asked.

Melvin leaned in close and started telling me how he'd broken up with his last girlfriend for being too fat and how he couldn't wait to get to know me. WTF?!?

The waitress set my glass of wine down, and I chugged it.

"What are the chances of me seeing the inside of your apartment tonight?" he asked, in what I can only assume he considered his sexy voice. He leaned even closer and slid his arm around my waist.

"Not gonna happen!" I yelped, unpeeling his arm and shoving it back at him. I looked at the rows of bottles behind the bar and came to the realization that there was not enough booze in this bar—or possibly the world—to make this guy palatable. I got up and walked out.

Back in the dark days, prior to meeting *moi*, my boyfriend was helping his now-ex celebrate her birthday. They were at a bar; he decided that she needed a special birthday taco (not a euphemism—I'm talking the traditional Mexican treat) and set out to get her one.

Except he was so drunk he passed out on the subway and wound up three boroughs away in the Bronx, nary a taco in sight when he returned four hours later.

At least if you date a drinker/drugger you won't have to worry about being bored because you'll always have your

Al-Anon friends to keep you busy. Plus, drunks are nothing if not completely unpredictable.

But don't be the drinkypants dater. A pre-date glass of wine to kill the jitters is fine; anything more than that, you may find yourself cruising unfamiliar, far-away, neighborhoods on a futile quest for Mexican snack foods. Or worse!

THE FACE OF EVIL

Just like some people are too stupid to date, some people are just too evil. There are far too many of them out there if you ask me, and I don't know why they don't just stay sequestered in their apartments keeping their nasty all to themselves. But I guess if you're a heinous slag of misery, you're far too awful to do anything so nice as not inflicting it on others.

My friend Rich—you may remember him from earlier— has a bad habit of finding the crazy and the creepy. As I've known him for a few years, I'm pretty immune to his stories, but Yovanne had even me shrieking "NOOOO!"

"She told me upon meeting me for the first time that my penis was obviously too small for her, and I would have to get a penis enlargement," he told me as I choked on my beer.

"But, but, but . . ." I protested.

He shot me a look. "No, she hadn't seen me naked yet," he answered my unasked question. "We'd just met. She said she just knew it, from *the way I walked*." (Emphasis mine.)

Despite the fact that this woman was a bitch of epic proportion, Rich still went home with her, where the humiliations just kept piling up.

"During sex—little-dicked sex, one would assume—she kept complaining, 'I can't feel anything!' All the while I was thinking, 'Tough shit, I can,' and ignored her. That went on for some time until she finally said, 'Hey, I think I felt something that time.'"

Dear sweet baby Jesus! I am going to fly down to North Carolina and put a lock on Rich's computer *and* his underpants.

Twenty-seven-year-old photo editor Lindsay has also had experience with the shockingly sadistic. "We went out to dinner first, and he drank so much at dinner, he was starting to get incoherent. Then we went to a bar—I wanted to go to one by my house so I could leave once I was done with my one drink.

"I drank it and told him I was going to head home. He offered to walk me home." By this point her date was stumbling, shit-faced drunk.

"I said no big deal, it was a block. And he was like, no, no, no, let me walk you home. I didn't want him to know where I lived because he was *that* creepy."

Lindsay's date tried to put her on the defensive by accusing her of not trusting him. "It was so creepy for him to ask that, so I said no, I don't. This is the first time we've ever gone out. You have to earn that."

Upon hearing that, her date went round the bend and started yelling and pointing and making a scene: "You're just like all the other women in New York. You've been hurt before, is that it? You can't let anyone come in and be a good guy, you have to question everything!"

Lindsay decided she'd had enough, grabbed her coat, and turned to leave. "Then he stuck his foot out and tripped me down to the ground!"

Jesus. "I was so pissed, I started yelling at him, 'What are you, eleven?!?' Then he tried to trip me again! He was a complete freak. What a weirdo."

Lindsay eventually escaped and called a male friend on her way home. When she told him what had happened *he* started yelling, "You have to call the police! Where is he— I'll kill that guy!" She told him she appreciated his concern but doubted that the police would be interested in some guy who'd tripped her.

Silence on the other end of the phone. Oops. Her friend thought she'd said the guy had *raped* her!

DON'T BE THAT DATER

If a good day for you consists of drowning a litter of puppies or shoving a blind man into traffic, do the rest of the world a favor and stay home. Consider celibacy. Paint an ugly picture, punch a hole in your bathroom wall, or write a crime novel. Just please don't inflict yourself on others.

How Not to Date a Stripper

Trixie (fake name!): Various NYC early nineties–era strip clubs (i.e., a time before silicone balloons were a job requirement)

What's the biggest misconception people have about strippers?
That we're horny, stupid, and love men. Also, they tend to think that we were all sexually abused. I wasn't and I knew lots of nice girls who weren't.

What's the exact wrong way to try and pick up a stripper?
Handing them a hundred-dollar bill with your number inside, because then it makes you look like you're looking for a hooker. That will get you a hooker, but it's no good if you're trying to date someone. Any time money was offered in exchange for services . . . that wasn't going to end well for them.

What's the lamest pickup attempt you ever suffered through?
One guy gave me a cocktail napkin on which he'd scrawled "Your 2 good for this. Call me enytime." I resented that because it was grammatically ill-conceived, riddled with misspellings and plus, how did he know I wasn't just some stupid whore—I might've been injecting heroin into my gums. I think that being a brunette with small boobs made me seem smarter.

Did you date guys you met at work?
Yes.

How about one of the regulars—someone who came in every day?
Actually, I did date one of them because he was really good looking in that WASP-y way that makes me crazy. But he turned out to be a mess. He was looking to be stepped on and wound up being abused by two women who used him to open their own strip club in Queens and then they siphoned all the money. I think he had self-esteem issues, despite being a really handsome, successful banker.

A strip club definitely breaks down barriers—it's easier to talk to people in a strip club. The women are encouraged to socialize and the men are certainly open to it so there's no hidden agenda.

Did you see any difference between the men who hit on you when you were a stripper and then when you had regular jobs?
None. It was just a slower process. They all want to get laid.

How has your opinion of men changed pre- and post-strip club?
They're more likable now that I'm out of the strip club. Although it was quicker work when I was dancing—you could always tell who the doofuses were right away. Whereas if I'd met them in an office, it might take longer to figure that out.

I know you met two long-term boyfriends at work—how did that work out?

They always hated it. They both ended up resenting it and were embarrassed by it. One boyfriend—we'll call him Chuckles—I think he resented it because it was easy money and he couldn't do it. I'm sure it was in their mind that if I'd met them there, then I could easily come up with a replacement there. One of them was a snob and was embarrassed to introduce me to his friends. He wouldn't tell people how we met. After I quit, post-breakup, he said, "that's all I needed you to do."

Oh, please! He went into the relationship knowing you were a stripper!

I know! And I enjoyed it. It was fun and I didn't appreciate someone trying to guilt me out of it. I knew I wasn't going to be doing it forever.

The other guy used to get pissed off when I'd bust out my tiniest G-string—which I called "The Moneymaker"—later at night when everyone was drunk. That used to make him so mad. That and when I'd roll my G-string down my hip. It wasn't like anyone was seeing anything new, but you have to give the guys in the audience the illusion that you're turned on by them. Plus, since I only had six sets a night I needed to maximize my time on stage.

I'M MAD AND I'M NOT GOING TO TAKE IT ANYMORE: ADVENTURES IN DATING THE TERMINALLY ANGRY

Unlike the Face of Evil, the Angry Guy/Gal probably won't take out their anger on you. At least not at first.

Instead, you'll bear witness to them freaking out over the most minor inconveniences. The fact that the bathroom is on the lower level—obviously put there just to inconvenience them. It's raining—again, the skies have opened specifically to ruin their new 'do. Like some sort of ill-mannered superhero, these types can see through the most banal comment and read insult into it. "Great shirt" becomes "all your other shirts are ugly and make you look fat." Angry people will imagine dirty looks where there are none and redefine paranoia for you. And just as a matter of fact, men seem to be about thirty-five times more likely to fall into this category.

Jill C., a Brooklyn-based saleswoman, had the bad luck to be out with one such maniac:

We were going out to dinner in a neighborhood that is notorious for never having available parking. We drove around for a few minutes and came across a car which appeared to be leaving the space. We waited for a few seconds, and when the woman would not acknowledge Tom [her date] or the fact he was waiting for the space, he proceeded to get annoyed and complain that she was rude, a racist. I should explain that Tom is black, and the woman was white. I told him that it was not that serious and he should relax. He yelled at me, saying I was "not on his side."

We finally parked the car and walked in silence. After a block or so, he turned to me and asked me something about the restaurant we were going to go to. I made a joke—which is what I do—about him playing nice from here on. He got upset and told me that he was "making amends" and I had to "start him up again" with my comment.

If that wasn't bad enough, we got to the restaurant and had to wait for a table at the bar. I ordered a drink, as did he, but Tom, being a pretentious fuck, ordered some drink that he was introduced to when he went to Brazil.

Apparently, this drink—I don't recall what it was called—required a special alcohol. The bartender brought our drinks, and Tom proceeded to get really angry since the drink was not the one he wanted. He called the bartender over and, in a really patronizing tone, asked her about it. She admitted they didn't stock the special alcohol, so he then asked for another drink, which she also screwed up. He gritted his teeth and asked me if he was "wrong" for getting upset. I told him that he didn't want my opinion, based on the fiasco in the car, and he started yelling at me again!

Obviously Jill never went out with him again, though not for a lack of trying on Tom's part.

DON'T BE THAT DATER

Have you ever punched a wall? Or a person? Do you frequently fly into rages? Do people seem like they're afraid of you? If you answered yes to one or more of these questions, you might be an angry jerk. The terminally furious need more help than a how-to dating guide can provide.

THE GUN JUMPER

Obviously, there is nothing funny about stalking. Hacking into your date's e-mail, following him or her home, intercepting phone calls—all wrong, wrong, wrong. Stalking is not only a dangerous thing that should be discouraged at all costs, but also a big, fat dater don't. Which is why we're going to discuss the warning signs that you might be dealing with the brand of unstable who'll have no qualms about crossing that line.

Michelle thought she was doing a good deed when she set a friend of hers up with a guy she'd gone out with once. The friend—we'll call her "Jill"—and the dude—we'll call him "Travis Bickle"—went out a few times and seemed to be hitting it off. Until he showed up for their fourth date with J-I-L-L tattooed across his knuckles.

Jill quickly made use of the E-X-I-T.

I almost feel bad using another one of his stories, but Rich is a gold mine and besides, he gave me permission.

"How about the woman who showed up for our first date, handed me a Viagra, and said we'd need it in thirty minutes," he told me. Um, if a guy had done the equivalent, I would've left. But Rich is heartier—and apparently

175

hornier—than I. Besides, this was "vacation date," someone he'd hooked up with during a brief visit to NYC. What could possibly go wrong?

He continued, "She drove us to some hotel in Queens, whipped out the credit card; we went upstairs (where I did my Viagra best) and then started talking about how she'd love to move to North Carolina and how I should start looking for houses that were big enough for me and her and her kids."

Predictably, Stella Stalker wasn't quite done with Rich after the Viagra wore off and he had toddled back home to North Carolina. "She called about six times a day for the next three days. When I finally talked to her and told her it wasn't going to work out, she broke down in tears because I 'broke off the engagement.'"

If Rich wasn't lucky enough to have several hundred miles separating himself and Ms. Stalker, you can bet she's the type that would've shown up at his office, all tears and histrionics, demanding "closure." From there, it's only a short jump to a GPS device planted on your car's undercarriage and a mailbox full of magazines you never in a million years would've subscribed to.

DON'T BE THAT DATER

When you've been dating for a while, it's exciting when you finally meet someone who seems really different and great. But do your best to keep a grip on your enthusiasm; it's best not to leap on them from a thousand different directions. If you find yourself losing your mind over someone you've only met a few times, it's time to take up a hobby like basket weaving—or maybe begin a course of intense psychotherapy.

THE CHEAPSKATE, LEVEL IV

Remember Marissa and Clay—he of the girly hands? Another issue Marissa had was Clay's alleged cheapness. At least that's how she saw it. Marissa and Clay both made a lot of money. About halfway through their ill-fated date, I got a call from Marissa, who was phoning from the ladies room of the restaurant they were dining at. "He's making me pay for dinner!" she hissed.

I was confused and asked her to explain. "The check came, I offered to pay half, and he accepted!" she snapped. I pointed out that it didn't exactly sound like he was *making* her do anything and that if she didn't want to pay, she shouldn't have offered. Marissa hung up on me. See why we're not friends anymore?

Rachelle, a 35-year-old Amsterdam-based writer, now happily married, had a date with someone I consider to be the height of extreme cheapitude. If there were a skinflint Oscars, this guy would be going home with a statuette.

"I was out on this date—a first date, I might add," she told me. He'd taken her to dinner, and she was starting to like him as he leaned in for a passionate kiss. "After a little making out, I told the guy I was going home."

Her date had other ideas. "'I spent $150 on dinner and now I'm going home with blue balls?!?' he complained and kind of demanded!" The sad thing was, Rachelle was very used to paying for herself and, in fact, had offered. He'd refused, in favor of her reimbursing him via her vagina. That she preferred to use MasterCard to pay for her steak was not acceptable.

DON'T BE THAT DATER

There are women (and men) you can make a sex-for-cash transaction with. These people call themselves sex workers and will generally run you more than an order of beef Wellington and a glass of merlot. Oh, and they generally don't barter sex for food either.

THE CONSOLATION DATE

Michael and I were out on our third date when I noticed something was off. He was an actor I'd seen on *Law & Order* and had seemed like a genuinely nice guy on our first two outings. But like I said, he was acting kind of distracted and miserable this time, which is why I was so happy to run into my friend Susan and her date. The four of us sat together, nursing our beers and chatting. Susan's friend also worked in film, so he and Michael had a lot to talk about. Most of it involved the dropping of famous names, and so Susan and I may have been rolling our eyes just a bit.

How Not to Date a Porn Star #2

Joanna Angel: Founder of Burningangel.com, and
star/director of *Joanna's Angels* and many others

What's the biggest difference between the pick-up techniques men used back when you were just Joanna and now that you're a porn goddess?
It's been completely different. There's definitely a protocol of questions that people always ask. It's always the same thing. They want to know, "so are you like really coming on camera or is it just an act?"

They try to make it sound not sleazy, but it is. A lot of guys act like they're not fazed by my celebrity, but don't talk to me like a normal person. After they ask if I'm faking, they ask what my family thinks and if size matters.

They wonder if I enjoy it or if it's just for the money. I tell them that if I were a doctor or professor they wouldn't be asking questions like that. When I'm on a date I don't like to be treated like I'm on an interview. It's weird when you're on a first date and someone asks about your family–that's not small talk, that's what you ask after you know the person for a while!

I don't think they get that every single person asks me the same questions.

Do porn stars ever date civilians or do they stick with each other?
I've found that I connect to rock stars—just because they get treated the same way. I've found that a lot of rock stars—what they really want—is someone they can have a normal conversation with. Not about work, just about movies. Or food.

And that's what I want—someone I can talk normally with. Not just me talking and the other person listening.

What would you say is the ultimate Joanna Angel turn-off?
My ultimate turn-off is if someone is really close-minded. Racist, really religious . . . stupid idiots in general. Especially guys. Sometimes when girls are stupid it's kind of cute, but when guys are stupid, it's really annoying.

Do you think your "type" has changed since you started doing porn?
Definitely. I know this is going to sound weird, but guys should know this. Ever since I started doing porn, I care more about the guy's personality than I ever did. Actually having a physical connection with someone . . . I think it's very common. A lot of people will date someone for a while just because the sex is good. But there's not a lot of bad sex in my life, so actually having someone to connect with is really important to me. I can't date someone with no physical chemistry, but that part isn't as important.

Any fashion don'ts you can think of?
Tribal tattoos around the arm are a no-no. Get it removed. I don't think I could get past that and it's getting really hard because a lot of people have them. I could be friends with a guy with a tribal tattoo, but I don't think I could ever date him.

Also, guys with long hair who wear it in a ponytail. I've seen guys with long dreads and that's cool. But when a guy has that long ponytail hair—gross.

Would you prefer a potential date had or hadn't seen any of your films?
I kind of like it. I'm an egomaniac and a lot of the movies that I'm known for, I also directed. So when a guy has seen *Joanna's Angels*, I like that. I take pride in what I do.

So many guys tell me they can't watch my movies because they think it's going to make them sound better, but I know that they do. I think it's kind of hot. I'm flattered.

Have you ever been a bad date?
There was one Valentine's Day that I went out with this guy to a really nice restaurant. He had liked me for a while, but I was "eh" about him. I was single at the time and seeing a bunch of different people.

It just so happened that someone else I was also quasi-dating worked at the restaurant we ended up at. The guy who worked there was the one that I really wanted to be with. I was doing a lot of chasing with him.

We kept staring at each other all night. It had been a while since we'd had sex, and I just wanted to walk by and tease him. I gave him this you-want-me-but-can't-have-me look on my way to the bathroom. But he followed me in, threw me against the wall and we had sex. I hadn't planned on having sex with him in the bathroom! So I felt bad and went home with the first guy and had sex with him too because I felt guilty.

While I was with him, the guy from the restaurant kept calling and texting, and so I told the guy I was with that I didn't feel good and instead went over to the other guy's house.

I think everyone is entitled to one night like that.

Then Susan's date excused himself to the restroom, and Michael moved in on Susan. While he wasn't my boyfriend by any stretch, it was still fairly ego-deflating to watch as he hit on my friend. The fact that he had to *lean over me* to do it made it ten times worse.

"You're so beautiful," he told her. "You could do better than *him*."

Hey! What about me?! Aren't *I* beautiful?!?

Apparently not, as he kept up with the gushing until Susan's date returned. To her credit, Susan didn't look remotely flattered by his attention. I was mortified, and the two of them made their excuses and left.

Michael then turned to me and snippily quipped, "I don't want to date you."

No shit!

I told him that there were kinder ways to make that clear that didn't involve scamming on my close friends and then legged it home in a huff.

David, the reformed Leg Humper (see Part Three), also fell prey to the public dismissal. "I was semi-dating this crazy, high-strung Dominican chick," he told me. "One Friday night she calls me up and says she's going to kill herself. So I'm on the phone with her for three hours. I'm not her boyfriend, but

I help her out. The next day I buy her some roses and take her to this Mexican place that we both liked."

David got up to use the bathroom.

Just a brief aside—please note that bad things seem to happen when people use the bathroom. Now back to our regularly scheduled rant:

"When I came back, there was a guy standing over the table, massaging her shoulders! And he has this look on his face like 'I'm massaging your girl.' I sit down and ask her what's going on—while he's still rubbing away! She goes, 'We started talking and he got up and started giving me a massage.'"

Wisely, David got up and left.

DON'T BE THAT DATER

Richard, an LA-based filmmaker, was *that* guy. "Living in LA, you get really sick of dating models and actresses," he told me. I totally understand because I had a similar problem with stunningly handsome professional rugby players. *¡No más, por favor!* Ahem.

"So a friend fixed me up with this really hot Asian therapist, and we were maybe ten minutes into the conversation when I learned that she wanted to leave therapy to be an actress."

Richard groaned on the inside but checked out his surroundings on the outside. "Throughout the date, I'd been trading looks with a tall, vaguely foreign-looking woman sitting alone at a table. When the soon-to-retire shrink went to the bathroom,"—see what I mean? If you want to salvage your relationship, *hold it in!*—"we chatted. Turned out she was just off the boat from New Zealand, quite liked the looks of me, had overheard the entire conversation, and slipped me her number . . . all this before my date returned."

At least the therapist/actress didn't have to witness her own humiliation, which is preferable to what David and I had to deal with. The moral of the story: If you're going to hit on someone other than the person you're out with, wait until they visit the can and then be quick about it!

THE CRAZY, LEVEL III

Crazy comes in all shapes and sizes, and as Heather, a Greenpoint-based blogger, found out, it also wears a variety of outfits. Listen to her story of a second date gone terribly twisted:

He met me at the subway, but he had a cold and didn't want to be out, so we went back to his apartment for a beer. We're talking and suddenly it starts to get creepy. There was no real living room, so we had to hang out in his bedroom. He opens the door, and the walls are painted lavender—ugly and very effeminate, but at the time, I didn't give it much thought.

First he told me he was pissing in empty 40-bottles for a week. It didn't seem like there was any particular reason for this. The bathroom worked; he just preferred to pee in bottles and keep them around.

Then he opened this drawer and starts talking about his alter ego, Kiki. He roots around, pulls out a crotchless fishnet body stocking. Much to my horror, I realize I own the same body stocking!

Then he pulls out this little flogger with a Lucite handle on it. He starts examining it and remarks that it would probably fit quite nicely up someone's ass. I pointed out some cracks in the handle, which would

probably complicate such a maneuver. Long story made short, I made it a point to get out of there.

After I got home I gave my fishnet body stocking to the Salvation Army. I couldn't look at it without thinking of him wearing it.

DON'T BE THAT DATER

If you're a freak, wave that flag proudly. But please make sure you know your audience before you whip it out. I'm sure there are some girls who'd be proud to date a man that in touch with his feminine side. And I hear there are cults who drink their own urine. You just can't be busting all this wildness out on people unprepared for such things. That's how you end up getting included in books on bad dates!

THE INCONTINENT

N o, I didn't mean to write "impotent" (there are drugs) or "incompetent" (everyone has an off day): I'm talking about being out with someone who, for whatever reason, is incapable of containing their own waste. This has happened to Flavor Flav, and it happened to me.

Lisa from Manhattan also did her time with a Leaky Lou. "We met up for drinks on Cinco de Mayo," she told me via e-mail. "The night was going really well—we ran into some friends of mine and they liked him, and we got along swimmingly."

Never a big drinker, Lisa stopped after two beers but noticed that her date was really pounding them back. By the time they decided to go home, he was toasted. "He asked if we could split a cab and said he would drop me off first since I lived the closest."

The two cabbed it to Lisa's, where she got out and said good night. As she walked to her door, she heard someone call her name. "The boy was standing on the street—the cab had driven away. He said he had to use the bathroom and could he come upstairs?"

Aaah, the old need-to-pee trick. Lisa was annoyed, but he seemed harmless and she let him in. "He tried to make out with me in the elevator. He was cute but *so* drunk, I wasn't interested in fooling around at that point. We made it into the apartment, and he went over to my bed and collapsed onto it, fully clothed, messenger bag and shoes still on, face down, snoring."

Lisa tried to push him out of bed, but he was down for the count. As it was already 2 a.m. and she needed to work the next day, she just climbed into bed with him.

At 4 a.m., she heard him stir. "I open an eye to see what's going on," she reported. "He climbs off the bed, takes off all of his clothes, and stands at the foot of my bed, buck naked. Then he proceeds to wander around my apartment for a minute or so. The next thing I see—and hear—is him *peeing* on my bed, my dresser, the window-sill, the rug, the closet door, and then finally making it into the bathroom."

But Lisa's night in hell wasn't quite over yet. "I hear a loud 'THOOMP!!!' indicating that he must have passed out inside. I can't believe what I just witnessed, so I fly out of bed, throw some sandals on, and turn on all the lights in the apartment."

Try as she might, Lisa couldn't get the bathroom door open. No doubt due to her date being passed out in front of it. So she began pounding on the door as hard as she could. "Boy comes out naked and squinting and looking totally confused. Without saying a word, I grabbed his clothes and bag, and shove them into his chest and push him out of the apartment and into the hallway—still naked."

Heh. "He called a few days later to apologize and to tell me that he left his necklace in my apartment. I said I would mail it."

As usual, I can top this tale. I met Anthony at the skankiest bar in my neighborhood. My buddy Eddie and I were drinking beer and no doubt discussing something of vital importance when his friend Anthony interrupted.

Anthony had a thick Bronx accent and spoke very slowly—kind of like he might've been dropped on his head at an early age. I noticed that despite his retard drawl, Anthony was actually kind of cute and bore a striking resemblance to my favorite Baldwin brother—Daniel, the fat, crack-smoking one.

Unfortunately, Anthony lived with his girlfriend. However, that didn't stop us from engaging in an everything but–type relationship. I did feel guilty about jamming my tongue down someone else's boyfriend's mouth, but I didn't let that stop me. Plus, as long as we weren't putting tab A into slot B, it wasn't *really* cheating. Or at least that's what Anthony kept assuring me.

But a couple months of extreme makeouts with no payoff started to make me cranky. At eighty-two days and counting, I hadn't waited this long to fuck someone since I was a virgin. I was losing patience quickly and decided to put some distance between us.

Then they broke up. Not because he couldn't live without my loving, nope. It was her. She got fed up with him and split town. I was elated, and the next time I ran into him, I dragged what I soon discovered was his very drunk ass home with me.

Excited does not begin to describe my mood. We got back to my house and immediately began ripping off each other's clothes with reckless (and drunken) abandon. Suddenly he stopped and excused himself to the bathroom. I took the opportunity to pop into the kitchen to fix myself a refreshing glass of ice water. I heard him lumber out of the WC and plop himself down on my bed. By now I was sporting a naughty little black slip (think Elizabeth Taylor in *Cat on a Hot Tin Roof*) and was ready—soooo ready!—to roll.

I sauntered back into the bedroom, striking what I believed to be a sultry pose in the doorway. As I paused for effect, I detected a smell—and not a good one. More like an odor. Much to my annoyance I noted that Loverboy was passed out facedown on my futon, legs hanging stiffly off over the side. The smell got stronger as I got closer. It was a foul, yet somehow organic stank.

It can't be, I thought to myself. But as my eyes adjusted to the lack of light, I looked down at his boxer-clad butt and saw a sight that no woman should ever have to see: a puddle of poo creeping its way out of his boxers and onto my sheets. I stood stock still in horror for a few seconds, and then I screamed. I poked, I prodded, I yelled some more, but I couldn't wake his poopy ass up.

Wringing my hands in disgusted, frustrated, mortified horror, I lay down on the sofa. I think it goes without saying that I didn't sleep a wink.

The next morning I heard him stir. "Oh shit," he exclaimed aptly in his retard drawl as he noticed that he'd crapped his pants. I squeezed my eyes shut and pretended to be asleep as he let himself out.

Unlike Lisa, I never got an apology. Linens were disposed of, the futon was bleached, and Mr. Poopypants never even apologized! I could think of nothing else for days but was way too mortified to tell anyone, though it was haunting me. Everywhere I looked, I saw his poopy butt. I knew I had to get it out of my system.

I phoned Eddie. "You have to come meet me. I need to talk to you in private," I implored. Eddie is lazy and tried to get me to spill over the phone, but I needed the support that only an in-person consultation could provide. He whined until I offered to buy him beer. He's also cheap, so this was my ace in the hole.

I met him at the same bar I'd left with Anthony a few nights prior. I purchased his carbonated alcoholic beverage and tried to get him to go for a walk so we could talk far away from prying ears. He insisted on staying put, so I located an out-of-the-way booth, swore him to secrecy, and solemnly told him what had transpired.

Anthony shit himself in my bed.

"What?"

You heard me. He crapped his pants. In my *bed!!!*

To say Eddie laughed is an understatement. He howled; he shrieked; he was so raucous in his merriment that bar patrons kept coming over so I could tell them the funny joke I'd obviously just told my friend. I was not remotely amused. The more I yelled at him to shut up, the harder—and louder—he laughed.

And I can't help but think it happened because I was messing with another woman's man. Karma's a bitch. And a smelly bitch at that.

DON'T BE THAT DATER

Did you notice the common denominator in both of these dates? Yep, once again, booze played a part in loosening sphincters and relaxing urethras. If you know you come undone when you imbibe, do your date a favor and invest in an adult incontinence garment. Or at least some paper towels or wet naps.

LIAR, LIAR, PANTS ON FIRE —THE DEEP END

Everyone stretches the truth at the beginning of a relationship. Mostly we're talking minor fibs along the lines of "No, really, I love spending Sunday afternoons quaffing domestic beer, scarfing nachos, and watching football with forty of your closest frat brothers!" or "Salma Hayek is like dog food next to you." What we're talking about here is the biggest lie of all—the M word.

If you can subtract ten pounds from your ass or add a couple zeroes to your income, just imagine how easy it is to pass yourself off as single within the forgiving confines of the online dating world. That must've been what Dr. Khaled Zeitoun, a married fertility specialist, was thinking when he seduced at least two women via the information super-highway. Unfortunately for the Bad Doctor, these two ladies not only caught on to his scam, but decided to sue him for breaking their hearts and telling lies. Zeitoun claimed to be single and is alleged to have used mind games and tales of past lives (WTF?) to lure them into having sex with him. No word on how his wife felt about these revelations, but the two women scorned are seeking unspecified monetary dam-ages for infliction of severe emotional distress "outside the boundaries of human decency and social norms."

The Internet has received a lot of bad press for the way it seemingly facilitates infidelity, but truth be told, would-be philanderers are everywhere. "I work in children's pub-lishing, and all the men there are either married or gay, so you tend to notice the young, cute straight guys," Lorelei, a young editorial assistant, shared with me. "This one guy was in another department that I never had any contact with—I'm telling you this because I have a rule about not dating people from work."

Lorelei's co-worker wore a pair of hideous glasses that he was very proud of. "I knew he loved his glasses, so I complimented him on them. One day he e-mailed and invited me to go buy glasses with him. I thought it was a date." Being a girl, she forwarded his e-mail to friends, and they all agreed it was a date.

The two walked around and did a little shopping, and Lorelei was having a good time until he asked her if she knew any places to find cute vintage women's clothing.

"I asked him why he needed women's clothing. And he answered, for his girlfriend. But—of course—he wasn't happy with her, they'd been on and off . . ." We've all heard that one, sister—I bet she doesn't *understand* him!

"By this point I didn't care. I just wanted to get it over with. He wants to go eat, but says he doesn't have any money. We go to this cheap hot dog place, and it turns out he has no money at all. So I ended up paying."

Lorelei paid the bill and left in disgust. "He couldn't believe I didn't want to hang out with him again."

DON'T BE THAT DATER

Unfortunately for my karma (see the Mr. Poopypants story), I have been on all sides of the cheater spectrum; mostly as the cheated upon, several times as the third party, but only once have I been the philanderer. Not to make any excuses, but the cheatee in that case was someone so horribly abusive and psychotic that I didn't even include him in this book because frankly, there's nothing remotely funny about a sociopath with violent tendencies. Cheating on him was stupid, but I can't say I even feel a thimble-size drop of guilt over it—I should've never agreed to go out with him in the first, second, or third place.

Cheating *with* some undeserving mook several or more times is another story, though. I still feel bad about that. And not just because he ruined such a nice set of sheets.

AFTERWORD

The reason I decided to write a book called *How Not to Date* is because, when you get right down to it, finding love only involves three elements: common sense, timing, and luck. Fucking it up, however, takes a multipronged approach.

Not to mention that—unless you're on one—bad dates are far more entertaining than good ones, at least for those who get to hear or read about them. But now that you've waded through the worst, I'm here to assure you that there *is* hope.

Cue corny soundtrack music. Even though I worry that talking about it will put the whammy on it, after all my gazillions of bad dates—poopers and all—I did finally wind up with a pretty sweet guy. And hey, he started off as a dating don't (see p. 22)! If I—someone who's done everything wrong you could possibly think of—could find love, it'll be a snap for you.

ACKNOWLEDGMENTS

Before I get into naming names, I want to extend a big wet kiss to anyone who ever went out on a horrible date and was kind enough to tell me about it. Your names were often changed (usually at your request), but I know who you are and cannot thank you enough.

I want to thank my dad, his bride, and my brothers for (hopefully) doing as I asked and never reading anything of mine that I hadn't cleared first (including this book). Sue, you're the best sis a girl could have. Thank you to all my lovely editors/friends over the years, especially Richard Martin, who first hired me as a columnist at the *Seattle Weekly*, and also Kate Crane, Bethany Clement, Andrea Reyer Cooney, Alex Zaitchik, and Jeff Koyen.

Julie Mason read this thing from beginning to end and provided copious notes that are actually far funnier than the book she was critiquing—thanks, Jules!

I owe Terence Maikels at Sasquatch Books for commissioning this thing, Bob Mecoy for ironing out the details, Kurt Stephan and Diane Sepanski for making it coherent, and Sarah Plein for making it look so pretty. Roger Gorman gets a big thanks for keeping me in health insurance and for being a flexible and understanding part-time employer/ pal. My incredibly talented, brilliant, and hilarious friends also helped loads with their encouragement and contributions: Rose Palazzolo, Lance Still, Sylvia and Julian Ander, Richard Schenkman, Heather Mulcahey, Carly Sommerstein, Valerie Frankel, Kurt B. Reighley, Rachel Goldberg, Ivan Lerner, Michelle Goodman, Rachel Kramer Bussel, Rich Giorgi, Diane Mapes, Bob Morales, Elisabeth Vincentelli, Darius James, Michael Gonzales, Michelle Rogalla, Tracey St. Peter, the Irish Kevins—Murphy and Ryan— and Ms. Debra Ziss, I'm talkin' to you!

Thanks be to Spyro for restoring my faith in men and Mabel and Inky for being the best furry buddies a lady could ask for. (And yes, I thanked my cats. Get over it.)

ABOUT THE AUTHOR

Judy McGuire writes a sex and love advice column called Dategirl for the *Seattle Weekly*, which the Catholic League singled out in its 2000 Report on Anti-Catholicism.

In addition to advising the lovelorn, Judy has also freelanced for a bunch of other publications, including *Bust, Paper, Time Out New York, New York Press, Men's Fitness*, and *Complex*, to name but a few. Because she is nothing if not a deep thinker, she recently wrote an essay on the delicate matter of holding in one's farts around a new paramour, which was published in an anthology entitled *Single State of the Union: Single Women Speak Out on Life, Love, and the Pursuit of Happiness* (Seal Press).

Besides writing (or, as one ex-boyfriend called it, "typing"), Judy has garnered production credits on a number of true-crime

TV shows, scribbled rather boring (but remarkably well-paying) marketing copy, and worked as an ethnographer on a NIDA-sponsored anthropological study of heroin users in New York City. For one enchanted summer in the '80s, she even folded T-shirts at the Short Hills Mall Gap store.

Judy McGuire was born in New Jersey and is woman enough to say so. (Though you'd have to pay her a lot of money to go back there.)

Like everyone and their great aunt, she has a blog: www.dategirl.net.

HOW NOT TO DATE